I0153007

The 30 Day Home Management *Project*

How to Turn Chaos to Order on Day One

by K.S. Brixey

"Faith, Hope, and Love, and the greatest of these of is Love." – 1 Cor 13:13

May you have a strong Faith, renewed Hope, and True Love. K.S. Brixey

©2009 K.S. Brixey , Spiral Bound

©2011 K.S. Brixey, Kindle Edition

©2015 K.S. Brixey, Kindle 2nd Edition

©2016 K.S. Brixey, Trade Paperback

All rights reserved. No part of this book may be reproduced or utilized in any form or by any means, electronic or mechanical, including photocopying, recording, or by any information storage and retrieval system, nor shall it be translated into another language or otherwise copied for public or private use, excepting brief passages quoted for purposes of review, without permission in writing from the publisher. Inquiries should be addressed to R4CR Productions, 4000 W 6th Street, Suite B134, Lawrence, KS 66049.

This book contains the opinions and ideas of its authors, and is intended to provide helpful information on the subjects it discusses. The authors and publisher are not rendering personal medical, counseling, pastoral, or legal services through this book. You should always consult with your personal medical, counseling, pastoral, or legal professionals before making any decisions for yourself or anyone else with a specific problem.

Published by R4CR Productions, 4000 W. 6th Street, Suite B134, Lawrence, KS 66049

ISBN-13: 978-0-9793020-6-0

ISBN-10:   0-9793020-6-4

Special thanks to Amanda Guilfoyle at Remember When Photography, Ottawa, Kansas for helping with the book's cover and design.

DEDICATION

Dear Amanda,

I wanted to teach you every-thing you would ever need to know about running a house-hold but you grew up faster than I could learn. I started this book during those turbu-lent teen years when we had a hard time communicating but I still so longed to continue teaching you. This book is my gift to you. I hope it will help you run an efficient home with lots of free time to play with your kids and pursue the Big Dreams God has put in your heart.

All my Love,

Mom

Table of Contents

DEDICATION..3

INTRODUCTION 9

Instructions for the 30 Day Project 10

Day One

PROACTIVE PRAYER COVERING 13

Day Two

FUNCTIONAL ZONES 18

Day Three

HOUSEHOLD PROVISIONS 23

Day Four

KEEPING TRACK 29

Day Five

DAILY ROUTINES 35

Day Six

HOUSEHOLD FILES 43

Day Seven

PAYING BILLS 51

Day Eight

PERSONAL CARE 58

Day Nine

ESTATE PLANNING 64

Day Ten

SPIRITUAL NUTRITION 70

Day Eleven

HOUSE RULES 75

Day Twelve

PERSONAL SPACE 83

Day Thirteen

FAMILY READINESS 88

Day Fourteen

DELEGATING RESPONSIBILITY 93

Day Fifteen

HOME REPAIRS 99

Day Sixteen

FAMILY COMMUNICATIONS 103

Day Seventeen

STEWARDSHIP 107

Day Eighteen

HEALTH RECORDS AND PLANNING 114

Day Nineteen

DECISION MAKING 118

Day Twenty

INDIVIDUAL DEVELOPMENT PLANS 123

Day Twenty-One

HOME VISION 129

Day Twenty-two

ACTIVITY SPACES 136

Day Twenty-Three

HOME SECURITY 139

Day Twenty-Four

OUTSOURCING 144

Day Twenty-five

RELATIONSHIPS 149

Day Twenty-Six

PRACTICING GIFTS 154

Day Twenty-seven

HOSPITALITY 159

Day Twenty-eight

SLEEP AND REST 164

Day Twenty-nine

MASTER PLANNING 169

Day Thirty

MINISTERING TO OTHERS 174

Forms and Samples 179

   The 30 Day Project Schedules 179

      Chapter Two Functional Needs Index 181

      Chapter Four Samples and Forms 180

      Chapter Five Samples and Forms 184

      Chapter Six Filing Index 188

      Chapter Seven Samples and Forms 189

      Chapter Eight Samples and Forms 190

      Chapter Eleven House Rules 191

      Chapter Twelve Personal Space Balance Chart 193

      Chapter Twenty Individual Development Plan 194

      Chapter Twenty One Forms and Lists 195

      Chapter Twenty Two: Activity Balance Wheel.........................198

NOTES 199

About the Author 201

INTRODUCTION

Whether you are a stay at home mom with six kids or a working man or woman without children, it's not hard to feel overwhelmed by the demands of managing a home. The 30-day project is designed to help you move from chaos to functional in six weeks. You'll feel more peace about your home starting with Day One and as you move through the program your home's efficiency will dramatically increase. Because the program meets you right where you are, you can repeat the six-week program as many times as you need to until you've reached a highly efficient level of home management. At that point, a two-week review is included to keep you and your home at a high level of readiness. Recapture your home's joy and your peace of mind.

Instructions for the 30 Day Project

Step One: Home Management Notebook

Dedicate a ½" 3-ring binder for project notes and to become your Home Management Notebook.

Step Two: Time

Schedule some time to complete the project goals.

Each chapter is broken down into one of the 30 Home management areas, determine to spend 15 minutes five days a week, such as Monday-Friday, reading one chapter each day and establishing a goal in that home management area. If you have more time, you can get started and often accomplish your top priority goal in that area the same day.

Determine to spend three to four hours one day of each week, such as a Saturday morning, accomplishing the goals you have set in each of the five areas that week. You can also use the time to work on goals set in previous weeks.

Write down your schedule and put it in your Home Management Notebook.

Step Three: Prioritize

After each chapter, answer the 30-Day Project review questions. List your area goals in your Home Management Notebook. Write down your top one or two goals for each project area in your Home Management Notebook.

Step Four: Goals

If you have time during your weekly review, start or complete your number one or two goals in that area or you can spend the time planning what you will need to accomplish your goals during the time you've set aside to complete projects this week. To make the most of your project time, schedule a time to gather or shop for materials for all five of this week's project areas before your project time begins.

Step Five: Projects

Prioritize your list of the top goals for each of the week's five project areas. Complete as many as possible during your allotted project time.

Step Six: Rest

Take a day off for rest, worship, and family time.

Step Seven: Continue

Continue through five project areas each week; complete as many of your top goals in each area as possible. At the end of six weeks, take time to list all that you have accomplished in your home management notebook and the differences you have noticed in the functionality, efficiency, and enjoyment of your home.

Step Eight: Finish

Take a week or two off to enjoy what you have accomplished and to finish up some of the tops goals that you were not able to complete.

Step Nine: Repeat

Start the project over at Day One. Each time you go through the project you will improve the functionality and efficiency of each project area. Repeat the 30-Day project until you feel the majority of project areas are functioning at high level of efficiency.

Step Ten: Review

Once you have reached a high-level of home management efficiency, in order to maintain that level, you can increase the interval at which you complete the 30-day project, such as once or twice a year or utilize the 2-week review four to six times a year. The two-week review covers three project areas a day, five days a week, for two weeks. It follows the same structure as the thirty day project but assumes that your goals will be less intense so you can cover three a day instead of one. In both cases, you have more time in between reviews to complete your goals.

Day One
PROACTIVE PRAYER COVERING

"Each one had a harp and they were holding golden bowls full of incense, which are the prayers of the saints."

Revelations 5:8 (NIV)

"I am going and you can't stop me," my seventeen year old daughter yelled as she stormed out of the house and disappeared into the darkness. She had made up her mind she was going out whether I approved of her friends or not.

I knew my daughter was right. I could not stop her from going out if she was determined to go against my wishes. My insistence had failed and I could not physically restrain her. All I could do now was pray.

"Lord, please keep her safe," I cried.

This was not the first time I prayed similar prayers; "My child is in a desperate situation, Lord, please help!" I can recount many times I prayed for my family to be rescued from bad situations; like when my seven year old was having adjustment problems in first grade or the trailer tire blew out in the middle of an unfamiliar metropolitan area at dusk. I have prayed over plumbing issues that even the experts could not fix, impending financial disasters, relationship conflicts, and many other home management issues. I began to wonder if a day would go by without a crisis to pray about.

You may already have a reactive prayer life for your home and, like me, can testify to God's divine intervention in desperate times. I am very thankful that God intervened in this situation. Shortly after midnight that night my friend called to let me know my daughter was safe with her. God has never left me alone in times of crisis but I know that He wants there to be more in our relationship. As women and men who shoulder the responsibility for our homes, our families, and often our working lives, we want more than just surviving from one crisis to the next. We want God's presence fully in our lives. At some point I realized that my prayer life was all about crises and my time with God was always a desperate attempt to fix my kids or the plumbing or some other dire rescuing I needed. I was tired of living the chaotic life of a victim. It was time to begin a proactive prayer stance over my home and replace the urgency of my prayers with God's peace that transcends the chaos.

Proactive prayer is not a response to what has already happened but rather seeking God before anything happens. The difference between a proactive prayer life and a reactive prayer life becomes evident in our relationship with God. Reactive prayers are between a victim and her rescuer whereas proactive prayers elicit collaboration between friends. God has entrusted you with the care of your home and family and you can trust Him to show you the best way to do that.

When I watched my daughter walk off into the darkness, I was afraid and called upon God to rescue me. I didn't ask for my heavenly father's help until I had used up all my own resources. Why wait? When my daughter was two years old, I knew a time would come when she would begin to exercise her independence and that is when I could have started praying for her to make this journey wisely.

Do you have friends who contact you only when something is wrong? They speak with such urgency and energy about their own problems that there is no time to inquire about yours. In contrast, caring friends will call you up regularly just to hear your voice. There doesn't have to be a reason or a request to check in. I believe that is the relationship that God wants to have with us; a precious friendship where we contact him regularly and share our hopes and dreams for our home and family even when nothing is desperately wrong.

Maintaining friendships in our busy days can be difficult. Just keeping that weekly date with your spouse can be a challenge, well enough time with your close friends or if you are not married yet, working in time to pursue a relationship. If you have children, well, then you can multiply the challenge by the number of kids you have. You will also need to work in time for parents, siblings, and other extended family and friends. Do you try to squeeze in time with God around all that? When we put God first an amazing thing happens; God works out the time we need for everything else. He is like no other friend that we have. Make time with God and He can show you the most rewarding ways to spend the rest of your day, not just for your benefit but so you can be a blessing to those you make time for.

GETTING STARTED:

Begin a proactive prayer covering over your entire household. A wonderful way to do this is to start a prayer journal specifically for that purpose. In the front section of your journal, write down the names of each member of your family and those living in your house, your pets, and your address. You can also list any special concerns that you want to remember such as the ongoing plumbing problem or managing your finances. List all areas of your home life even areas that are going well. Write down your personal dreams and hopes for your family's future.

Establish a time block each day to spend in prayer. I have determined that the first fifteen minutes after I get home from work and the first fifteen minutes after I get up on the weekends will be dedicated to praying for my household. As I move through the house after work, I try to ignore the backpacks, dirty dishes, and things that would normally be subject to my barking out direct commands. No wonder the kids used to cringe when I pulled up in the driveway. Now, I pleasantly say hello, share a hug or two, and head back to my room to grab my prayer journal. I do make mental notes on the way; "Better put that on my prayer list, give this to the Lord, and that is definitely going to need some spiritual warfare." I say nothing aloud so the kids are safe for at least the first fifteen minutes after my arrival.

Designate quiet places where you can pray. In the summer, I like to spend my prayer time in the gardens or on the patio. In the winter, I often retreat to my bedroom for a little alone time or sometimes I pray at the piano while playing praise and worship songs. On the weekends, I will grab a cup of tea and curl up on the couch before the kids get up or head out on the deck to enjoy the sunrise. Just grab your prayer journal, a pen, and your bible and head to your favorite quiet place.

Although sometimes you may feel it is appropriate to invite prayer partners to join you, teach your children and let other family members know that this is your special time with the Lord. Let them know they will have your undivided attention when you are done.

Once you are settled in, look at your prayer reminders to help you get started. I often write out my prayers. Sometimes I read over prayers I have written in the past and pray them again until I get a clear answer. If they have been answered, I'll write out a prayer of thanks. Share with the Lord your concerns, personal dreams, and hopes for your home and family. Whether you write the prayer out in your journal or speak it aloud, use this time to bring anything and everything to the Lord concerning your household. Use the sample prayer or other prayer cards to get you started. You can also let scriptures or worship songs guide your prayers by personalizing your favorites.

Prayer journals, lists, and personalized scriptures are excellent tools to bring with you to your quiet place when you pray for your household. To keep your prayer time fresh have a lot of tools and quiet places to choose from but remember your relationship with the Creator is more important than the tools or the routines you use. The goal is not to spend fifteen minutes of the day confined to a specific sacred place to engage in a ritual prayer time but rather to make time to converse with your heavenly Father about your home and family. Enjoy this time with the Lord. Prayer is effective because it opens the communication lines that friends need to stay close. Talk to God daily. Don't wait for a crisis to go to Him. Share your heart with God, ask Him to guide you, and thank Him for being there in real and specific ways. Most of all, thank Him for calling you His friend.

SAMPLE: A Proactive Prayer over Your Home & Family.

"Lord, please open the door of my home to many family and friends. Make this place a refuge for your children and your lighthouse beacon to the lost. Let all who enter in feel welcomed, refreshed, and equipped with your power to face their daily battles. Let the love they find here remain dear in their hearts when they venture out into the world. Show me how you want my home to change and gently guide me in good stewardship of it. Mold me and make me a good friend to my brothers and sisters in Christ and to the lost. Lord, let my home draw people to your Light, let me be someone who illuminates your Love, and let all who cross my threshold be immersed in Your Presence. In Jesus name, Amen."

AFFIRMATIONS:
☐ I talk to God daily about my concerns and dreams for my home and family.

30 DAY PROJECT REVIEW QUESTIONS:

1. What does your current prayer covering consist of?
2. What do you like about your current proactive prayer routine?
3. How can you improve your current proactive prayer time?
4. List the goals you have for this area in your Home Management Notebook.
5. Choose one or two top priority goals from your list to accomplish or get started on this week. Write them in your Home Management Notebook.

TOOL KIT:

- ➤ Quiet place to pray.
- ➤ Designated times to pray.
- ➤ A prayer journal and pen.
- ➤ A list of reminders.
  - ☆ Names of family & household members
  - ☆ Name of family pets
  - ☆ Home management issues such as finances, stewardship, discipline, education
  - ☆ Dreams and personal goals
- ➤ Prayer helps
  - ☆ Scriptures
  - ☆ Praise and worship lyrics
  - ☆ Prayer cards

SUGGESTIONS FOR FUTHER STUDY:

- ➤ *The Power of a Praying Wife* by Stormie Omartian and accompanying prayer cards
- ➤ *The Power of a Praying Husband* by Stormie Omartian and accompanying prayer cards
- ➤ *The Power of a Praying Parent* by Stormie Omartian and accompanying prayer cards
- ➤ *The Power of a Praying Women* by Stormie Omartian and accompanying prayer cards

Day Two
FUNCTIONAL ZONES

"Well done, good and faithful servant! You have been faithful with a few things; I will put you in charge of many things. Come and share your master's happiness."

Matthew 25:21 (NIV)

Have you ever stepped into a busy first grade classroom? If that doesn't motivate you to get organized, I am not sure what will. How can one teacher get twenty children to keep all those small counting objects, crayons, markers, papers, and other materials neatly organized? While helping out in my son's first grade classroom I quietly observed these six and seven year olds working in small groups around the room. Some read, others counted math objects, and others were working in writing and drawing centers. There were kids and potential clutter everywhere.

I was amazed when the teacher said, "First graders, put away your materials and get ready to line up." After a few minutes of shuffling, not an object was left on the floor or the tables and twenty kids stood quietly in line awaiting further instructions. I thought to myself, "If I could tap into a fraction of that efficiency I would certainly be able to motivate four kids above the age of seven to pick up after themselves."

Looking around the room I noticed one of the keys to her success. Every item, down to the smallest counting bear, had a place for it to be when not in use. Every place was clearly labeled. Every area of the room was clearly zoned as to its function. When she said put away the counting bears, there was no doubt in the child's mind where the bears needed to be placed to finish her task. Everything in the room had a purpose. There were no boxes of papers left over from previous classes. No books waiting on the shelf for the children to use in sixth grade. No boxes of materials stacked to the ceiling that hadn't been opened since she started teaching twenty years ago.

These kids learned to sort in kindergarten and today that skill was paying off. All they needed was a system to sort and store items. This system worked because it only stored items waiting to be used again for a specific purpose during the first grade year. Notice I didn't say they were being stored in case a need arose in which the teacher might decide to use them for this class or for a future class. She only stored what they would use over the course of the current year.

GETTING STARTED:

In her book, "Organizing from the Inside Out," Julie Morgenstern suggests clearly defining the purpose of each room of your home. Begin with broad descriptions for each room and each area of each room. As you begin to bring purpose to the room and design each space, narrow your descriptions until each room, area, surface, cabinet, and drawer is defined by its function.

Drawing a map of your home including each room and outside areas can help you assess whether all your functional needs are being met. Make a list of the functions you need in your home such as cooking, dining, storage, and gathering with family members. Assign a room or an area of a room for each function. Then name each room with its intended function. As you start sorting, it may seem as if your things are determining your functional needs. For now, that is okay as long as you have room to define a place for each item. As God begins to reveal the true purpose for your home, your home's functional needs will define the things you keep in your home.

Now that you've identified some functional zones you can begin decluttering your house. "First graders, it's time to put away your materials." Use the simple skill you learned in kindergarten called sorting. You can do this in two ways depending on your current goal. Option one is to complete one room at a time by sorting its contents into their proper zones. This option works best if you have one room that you want decluttered immediately. Option two is to go through the entire house gathering items that belong in a particular zone and taking them there. This option works great if you are setting up a new zone or storage area and want all like items stored together. I find I usually mix and match both approaches.

Once you define a zone and start sorting, you will want to set up that space to function efficiently. This will include dividing the space up into more specific functions. Most people do this in the kitchen without much thought. You would not open a random drawer in the kitchen and toss the silverware inside. A specific drawer is designated as the silverware drawer. Even more specific is the slot in which you place the forks and the knives and the spoons. This is the same concept you will be applying to each room and space in your home.

When you first move into a new house, the boxes labeled "kitchen" are taken to the kitchen and those labeled "bedroom" are taken to the bedroom. Just as you would sort your moving boxes start sorting the things in your home to their assigned functional zones. You can stack things into piles or use and label moving boxes. Schedule a time to open boxes and eliminate piles by specifying a space for each item and putting each item in its place.

Solve organizational problems by reassessing the function of a particular space or defining a functional need not being met. Let's say you designate a corner of your closet to function as shoe storage. You start unpacking your boxes and gathering shoes from all over the house and pile them up in the designated space. Next, you want to organize them. You find out you have fifty pairs of shoes. You weed out those that don't fit and those you no longer want to wear. You have twenty-five pairs of shoes left in the closet. There is not enough room to lay out those shoes neatly so you go to the store and purchase a vertical rack that fits neatly in the given space and stores your twenty-five pairs of shoes. Now your shoe zone is neat and functional. You can easily see what shoes you have, will know exactly where your shoes go when you bring them to the shoe zone, and will be able see if any shoes are missing that need to be found.

THE PROCESS:

Life is going to begin to seem a lot less complicated now that you have designated your functional zones. As you walk through each room, you will recognize things that don't belong and be able to return them quickly to their correct zones. Even before you have each room set up to the detail of your silverware drawer, you will at least have a general area in which each thing you own belongs. Should you need to retrieve an item, you will know which area to look in. As you work on each zone your goal will be to know exactly which drawer, even which side of the drawer, an item is on.

Once your home is zoned your time is spent more efficiently because you are not searching an entire house for an item and you can solicit more help picking up because it is easy for helpers to quickly learn where things go. People are truly amazed when I can, to the exact corner of a specific drawer, tell my children where something is while I am in another state.

Once your things are sorted by zone, you may wish to design furniture and shelving systems to store and use your items efficiently in this functional space. This is when you will begin micro-zoning or assigning a function to the smallest spaces in which an item can placed. This doesn't have to be complicated. To this day I can tell you where my dad kept the fingernail clippers. Everyone in our house knew they were in the souvenir stein kept on the mantel and everyone knew they better be in there when my dad went looking for them. The goal of micro-zoning is that every item in your home will be stored in a specifically, assigned place for that item. Imagine the increase in your home's efficiency when you can find anything you need even in the dark.

Zoning is a continuing process. Take the time you need from the start to get your things sorted to the room level then set your priorities and start micro-zoning. Start with those areas that continually zap your attention and energy. Get into the habit of doing a little zone clean up whenever you walk through a room and you will be surprised how efficiently your home begins to stay clutter free and functional.

AFFIMATIONS:
- ☐ I have identified a place for every item in my home.
- ☐ I have a plan to help me keep every item in its assigned place.
- ☐ I have a plan to evaluate the efficiency of my functional zones and to modify them when needed. I will improve efficiency by narrowing the definitions of each zone as I use them.

30 DAY PROJECT REVIEW QUESTIONS:
1. What does your current system of zoning look like?
2. What is working with your current system?
3. What improvements need to be made to your zoning system?
4. List the goals you have for this area in your Home Management Notebook (HMN).
5. Choose one or two top priority goals from your list to accomplish or get started on this week. Write them down in your Home Management Notebook.

TOOL KIT:
> ➢ A list of possible functional needs for homes (Form 2-1).

> ➢ A list of your home's functional needs.

> ➢ A map of each room of the house and their zone assignments.

SUGGESTIONS FOR FURTHER STUDY:
> ➢ *Your Garagenous Zone: Innovative Ideas for the Garage* by Bill West
> ➢ *Organizing from the Inside Out* by Julie Morgenstern

Day Three
HOUSEHOLD PROVISIONS

"The wise, however, took oil in jars along with their lamps. ... The virgins who were ready went in with him to the wedding banquet. And the door was shut."

Matthew 25: 4 & 10

My husband loved to do the grocery shopping and he was good at it. He could walk through the grocery store and design meals using what he found on sale. He brought home a week's worth of groceries under budget and always paid with the cash in his wallet. I have a hard time making up an idea for a meal from the raw ingredients in the kitchen well enough imagine meals from in-store advertising. I never appreciated my husband's gift until it was up to me to take on the task of providing meals for my family after he died. For over twenty years I'd had it done for me, and now, it was up to me to do the grocery shopping and prepare meals for my family.

Initially, I tried my husband's method. I walked through the store, looked for the specials, and tried to think up meals centered on them. Although I took advantage of the specials, I spent much more than I budgeted for food. I had an advantage he didn't have; I had the opportunity to put my grocery tab on a credit card. That helped me not have to put anything back because I was over but it didn't help me get everything I needed. It never failed that when I got home to cook a meal I would be short an ingredient or I would not have an appropriate side dish to go with the meal. As a result, the kids and I ate a lot of fast food that first year.

In addition to problems in the kitchen, other problems surfaced such as desperate needs for toilet tissue or special trips to the store for one bottle of shampoo. Even when I made a list I either forget an item or over purchased an item I'd forgotten once before. One time my daughter would not eat the meal I'd prepared because we had no ketchup. So every time I went grocery shopping, thinking we were out, I would buy another bottle of ketchup. Soon we had enough ketchup to supply us for a few years but we ran out of mustard.

Things may not be this bad in your home but you know how frustrating it is to run out of something you need to finish a task such as running out of detergent at a time when one more load of laundry would mean you were caught up. If you are organized enough, you can buy that detergent when you can get the best price on it. Those dollars add up over the year. When you are buying things out of desperation, you pay a premium for them.

Another benefit to organizing the provisions for your home is that you will be able pull together a quick meal or prepare something to eat on the road in a few minutes. You don't have to prepare tofu to ensure the meals that come from your kitchen are better for your family than those that come from the fast food counter. Just eliminating the value meal soda drastically cuts down the sugar content and calorie count.

Organizing the provisions for your household will help you cut down on waste, allow you to offer healthier meals for your family, and help you complete household tasks efficiently. Keeping provisions on hand will save you money and time and help you be prepared for unexpected guests.

GETTING STARTED:

Let's start in the kitchen because everyone in your family eventually wants something to eat. In my house, it seems to be the first thing on their minds in the morning and the last thing on their minds at night. With four kids, you might guess there is always someone in the kitchen poking around looking for something to eat. My dad used to say, "A boat is just a hole in the water you throw money into," that sounds like my kitchen except the hole is in my kids' stomachs. I cart a lot of groceries into the kitchen and they seem to disappear before I get them put away.

Since shopping with a list has been found to be the most effective way to save money, we will prepare one. However, we won't start with the grocery list. We want to shop with purpose. Our first purpose is to prepare one evening meal per day for seven days. So we will start by preparing a list of seven main entrees for our Weekly Meal Plan.

List seven main dishes you know your family will eat and that you can prepare quickly. You can add to the list as you experiment and discover new family favorites. You can find new ideas on the back of soup cans and from the covers of frozen dinners. When possible, use double day. For example, my kids like Sloppy Joes and chili, so I will brown three pounds of hamburger, drain it, and scoop half of it into the crockpot and put half of it in the skillet. I make the sloppy joes in the skillet for the evening meal. Then I mix the rest of the chili ingredients in the crockpot with the other half and put the whole pot in the refrigerator to heat up the next day.

List seven side dishes you enjoy serving with the seven main dishes. I keep my side dishes simple because my kids can be very picky and I often end up being the only one eating an elaborately prepared side dish. Keep raw vegetables on hand like carrots or cauliflower and cans of fruits such as peaches or pears. Mix and match the fresh and canned side dishes with those that you prepare from scratch. A jar of applesauce or a container of cottage cheese will work well for a quick side dish. It's not necessary to plan each meal if you have a variety of side dish ingredients on hand and know what they are. Experiment until you find the seven sides your family loves.

When you are done with your 7's lists; 7 mains and 7 sides, take the time to write a corresponding grocery list that contains the necessary ingredients for each dish. Keep the list in your Home Management notebook. Once you get a sevens lists that works you can begin experimenting with a second one. I find that having a rotation of three to four sevens lists keeps home meals from getting boring. I also interchange my winter list, that includes hot and spicy foods like chili, for my summer list that includes a lot of outdoor grilling. Other helpful Kitchen lists include snack lists, breakfast items, lunch lists, beverage lists, and road trip items. Just keep these ongoing idea lists in your Home Management notebook under Household Provisions. You can refer to them as you make out your weekly meal plan and grocery store shopping list.

A road trip list consists of simple things you can throw in a picnic basket and cooler to make a meal on the road. If you keep these items in the pantry and freezer, you can throw together a picnic outing in minutes. Keep a jug of water in the freezer for your cooler. You may also like to keep something on hand for feeding and bedding down unexpected guests. I like to keep a box of hamburger patties and a package of hamburger buns in the freezer along with a large can of beans in the pantry in case a group of friends gather and I want to throw together a quick meal for us.

Now that you have a basic meal and grocery list, you can start making up your pantry inventory. This inventory will be used to make sure you have on hand everything you need to be prepared to cook in your kitchen. The pantry inventory includes ingredients for your 7 quick meals, your 7 side dishes, cooking and baking ingredients like sugar and flour, mainstays such as favorite family snack ingredients, breakfast items, lunch items, beverage mixes, and items from your road trip list. Use a needs list to mark down anything you have used up so you won't forget to stock up while you are at the store.

At this point, you know everything you need so it is time to go shopping. Gather your kitchen lists and inventories and transfer your needs list to the shopping list. Pull out your coupons for each item on your list and save even more money. If a main staple is on your list and it is on sale, buy two if you can. Stick to your list and avoid end caps unless they are on your list.

When you get home sort your ingredients into the quick meals you are going to make and put them in plastic grocery sacks sorted by meals; one for the pantry, one for the fridge, and one for the freezer. This helps in two ways—it lets your family members know that the ingredients have been set aside for a meal and secondly, it is very easy to grab a sack from the fridge and one from the pantry and you have everything you need to make the meal.

Other provisions in your home include hygiene items, cleaning supplies, and consumables such as light bulbs and paper products. Designate one place in your home to store these items until they are used. Then buy in bulk when they are on sale and store them. Keep an inventory list in your Home Management Notebook of what you need to have on hand and use your list to check off what you need when you make out your shopping list. Buying in bulk ensures you are ready for unexpected overnight guests as well.

As you clean your house or plan repairs and updates to your home, keep a list of items needed. This list should include the dimensions, color schemes, and regular prices you've seen for these items. Take the list along when you shop in case you find a listed item on sale – using your list you'll know if it will work for your project.

Always shop with a purpose and only spend your money with a plan in mind. Don't let end cap advertising or in store specials persuade you to buy. If it is not on your list, it is not a deal. However, a sale price for an item on your list is a special. In this day of excessive clutter, remember, "Less items of higher quality with predetermined purposes means more value for your life."

AFFIRMATIONS:
- ☐ I have a week of quick easy meals planned and a well-stocked kitchen to prepare them.
- ☐ I prepare my shopping lists at home and shop with purpose for quality and value.
- ☐ I am prepared with adequate household supplies and an inventory system.

30 DAY PROJECT REVIEW QUESTIONS:
1. What does your current household provision system look like?
2. What is working with your current system?
3. What improvements are needed for your current system?
4. List the goals you have this area in your Home Management Notebook.
5. Choose one or two top priority goals from your list to accomplish or get started on this week. Write them down in your Home Management Notebook.

TOOLKIT:
- ➢ **Kitchen Lists:**
  - ◷ 7's List: 7 Mains & 7 Sides & their ingredients
  - ◷ Lunch, Snacks, and Beverages lists
  - ◷ Road trip inventory list
  - ◷ Pantry Inventory List
  - ◷ Needs List
  - ◷ Grocery Store Shopping List
- ➢ Household **Supplies** Inventory List
- ➢ Discount and supply store shopping list
- ➢ **Home** repair and update lists
- ➢ Hardware and home maintenance store shopping list

SUGGESTIONS FOR FURTHER STUDY:
- ➢ *A Dinner a Day: Complete Meals in Minutes for Every Weeknight of the Year* by Sally Sondheim and Sazannah Sloan
- ➢ *The What's for Dinner Cookbook: 52 Weeks of Balanced Dinners for Your Family* by Kathleen Botta and Claire Mendonca.

- ➤ *Don't Panic Dinner's in the Freezer* by Susie Martinez, Vanda Howell, and Bonnie Garcia.
- ➤ *Make Ahead Meals* by Jean Par.

Day Four
KEEPING TRACK

"She watches over the affairs of her household and does not eat the bread of idleness."

Proverbs 31:27

"Service," the bright orange light on my thermostat read. We were on the brink of winter; this was not a good time for lights to begin appearing on the heating devices. I decided not to let it go and called out a professional to check it. He only charged me eighty dollars to determine that apparently nothing was wrong. "But what about the orange light?" I asked.

He thought maybe the thermostat was going haywire and if it happened again he would replace it. However, he assured me we would continue to have heat and was glad to see that I was keeping up the maintenance.

"Maintenance?" I asked.

"Yes, I see you've been changing the filter. It is important to keep the dust out of the blower motor." He explained.

"Good thing," I thought but I had to wonder who had been changing the filter. It had been over a year since my husband died and I didn't even know there was a filter behind that slice of sheet metal. Apparently, my husband had known because I later found a stack of new filters in the garage. There was a note written in black marker next to the filter door that said, "change monthly." The service man had explained that changing the filter monthly would keep the dirt out of the blower motor and help to stop allergens and other pollutants from entering the central air ducts.

I wondered how many more little tasks I had neglected since my husband died. I thought about things he used to do such as changing the oil in the vehicles and cleaning out the rain gutters. There are many items that need to be done around the home inside and outside. Some tasks are on going, some seasonal, but done regularly preventative tasks save money and headaches down the road.

One fall I didn't clean our gutters and ended up paying a maintenance company one hundred dollars to defrost ice off our heat pump during a winter storm. The leaves had clogged the gutters and rain water had overflowed onto the heat pump's outdoor unit and froze. The rain along with freezing temperatures had turned the entire back yard into an ice skating rink. The overflowing water that drained onto the heat pump froze solid stopping the fan from turning. The same technician, who slipped and fell on the ice in my backyard, pointed out the accumulation of icicles hanging above the heat pump. These stalactite-like formations were evidence that the gutters were not properly draining.

If we had had the task tracker for preventive maintenance I could have easily carried on my husband's maintenance tasks after he died without forgetting important tasks. I would have not found out the hard way about the need to check the tire tread before pulling a trailer down an interstate. I would have realized that the oil needed to be checked before the oil light came on and the engine froze up. I would have saved a technician a bad fall on the ice and the hundred dollars it cost me for him to thaw out my heat pump. A simple record of what maintenance had been done in our home would have given me a better idea of what I needed to accomplish in my husband's absence. I could have handed the maintenance list to anyone who said, "How can I help you?" during the months after he died.

GETTING STARTED:

To make things run smoother in your home you will need to develop a system to keep track of recurrent cleaning, maintenance, and preventative check ups for your house, appliances, and vehicles as well as preventative checkups for your family members' health, including family pets. See Appendix, List 4-1 for a list of common recurring household tasks. Refer to the operation or owner's manual for each appliance and vehicle you own to determine the recommended recurring tasks to include in your task tracker.

Subdivide your tracker into sheets of related tasks such as interior home, exterior home, outbuildings, health, or home office. Other tracker sheets can be used for keeping track of birthdays and systematic preparations for holidays. Keep your tracker sheets together in your home management notebook and use them to schedule tasks in your day planner as needed.

To schedule home maintenance on your tracker, begin by doing the task. Choose one of the common recurring household tasks from List 4-1 that you know you can complete right now. Do it. Then write it on the appropriate tracker form. Mark it as completed by placing an X on the task's line in the column corresponding to the current month. Check the frequency listed or your owner's manual to determine how often the task needs to be done. Highlight or darken around the square on the task's line that corresponds to the column under the projected month the task needs to be done next and all future dates for the current year. If the task frequency is greater than an annual, write the projected date due on the task's line under the future date column. For example, you took the dog in for his 2- year rabies shot. Put an X on the task line under the month you took him in and write the month and year the shot will be due again under the future date column. When you begin a new task tracker sheet next year, you will transfer these dates to the new sheet as appropriate.

Ref	Tasks	FRQ	J	F	M	A	M	J	J	A	S	O	N	D	Future Date
	Change filter in Heater/AC Blower unit	M	X	X	X	X									
	Clean out rain gutters	A										☐			

Ref	Tasks	FRQ	J	F	M	A	M	J	J	A	S	O	N	D	Future Date
Ginger	Rabies Shot	2yrs.				X									April 2008

Ref	Tasks	FRQ	J	F	M	A	M	J	J	A	S	O	N	D	Future Date
Taurus	Change Oil	Q			X		X			X					
Truck	Change Oil	Q	X			X			X			☐			

Sample 4-2: Task Tracker

The task tracker, sample form 4-2, is both a reminder and check off tool. A task comes due on the date marked with a square on the task tracker sheet but it may not actually be accomplished at that time. When the task is actually completed, put an 'X' in the square that corresponds to the month it was completed. For some tasks that is all you need. For example, the furnace filter is changed monthly and you just put an 'X' in the square on the tracker schedule to let you know it was accomplished. The same is true for other monthly cleaning tasks. If you miss a month on these tasks, you can't do them twice. I'll put an 'M' inside the dark square to show that I missed it.

For vehicle maintenance you may want a more comprehensive record, see sample form 4-3. You may want to start a separate record for each vehicle that includes things like the mileage at which the task was completed, what type of oil was used, what additional tasks were completed, who did the maintenance, and any comments the technician made. If your record of maintenance requires more than a checkmark and date, I recommend preparing a separate record sheet for that appliance, vehicle, or item. These sheets can be kept in your filing cabinet along with their owner's manuals or kept in your home management notebook. Be sure to list any forms you keep separately in your Home Maintenance Notebook's Index so you'll remember where to update your records.

Vehicle Year/Make/Model: *1996 Ford Windstar* VIN# _____				
Date	Odomet	Description of Maint.	Service Ctr/Tech	Mechanic's Comments
12-19-06	*65,499*	*Changed Oil 10W40 Penzoil & oil filter*	*Joe's Garage/ Bob*	*R. front tire tread wearing low*
1-6-2007	*65,610*	*Replaced two front tires w/ P125R17*	*D&D Tires/Mark*	*Tiger Paws*

Sample 4-3: Vehicle Record Form

You will be adding to your task frequency reminder list as we move through the 30-day project. For example, when we start talking about personal care you may wish to add tasks such as haircuts, every 6-8 weeks to your Task Tracker- Health sheet.

If you have not already done so, take a few minutes and walk through your home listing the make, model, year, and serial number of each major appliance you own, see sample form 4-4. Gather your owner's manuals together. We will be setting up a file for them on day six but for now designate a temporary gathering place and get them all together. As you flip through the manuals you can list the recommended maintenance and cleaning tasks on your tasks frequency list. If you have listed a major appliance and can not find your owner's manual, try to find the manufacturer's web site. Often they have listed the recommended maintenance and cleaning tasks for your appliance's make and model online. You may also wish to order a replacement manual. Don't forget to put your appliance inventory list in your Home Management Notebook or in your home filing cabinet under assets and maintenance records.

Make	Model	Year	Serial #	Warranty Expires	Task FRQ's	Purchase Info (Date/Cost/Whom)	Manual?
Sears-Dryer	KA1667	2001	498	12/14/2006	A	12/14/2001 Sears, Lawrence, KS	Yes

Sample 4-4: Major Appliance List

Although the task tracker is not an appointment calendar, it is important to check off the tasks you have completed. This way the scheduler can serve as a record of what has been completed. If for any reason you are not available, a friend or relative can come into your home and help accomplish necessary tasks for you. You will also be able to tell what tasks you are unable to complete and delegate them to another household member or pay a professional to complete them. I put a check mark by the task when I have made an appointment with a professional to do it and have written it in my day planner or appointment book. Then I put an 'X' through the checkmark when it is actually completed. For most tasks, this serves as an adequate record. For other tasks, like the vehicles, I do the same but additionally I fill out their individual maintenance record.

When will you accomplish these tasks? The accomplishment of tasks is two-fold and depends on whether this is a task you do yourself or one that requires scheduling with a professional. Set aside a block of time each week to review your Task Tracker. Make appointments for the tasks that are coming up that require outside resources such as a mechanic or doctor. For dentist appointments you generally have to schedule these three to six months in advance. Place a check in the square when these tasks are scheduled in your day planner or appointment calendar.

For other tasks decide whether to ask a household member for help or consider the length of time it will take you do them and block out a time during the next week to accomplish them. I recommended including time during this session to complete as many tasks as possible. I find it helpful to schedule blocks of time to accomplish these tasks just like I would make an appointment to have the oil changed or take the dog to the vet. The task tracker reminds you of what needs to be done and allows you to block out the time necessary to accomplish the task or hire someone to come in and complete it for you.

AFFIRMATIONS:

- ☐ I have a list of the required recurring tasks and their recommended frequency to maintain my home.
- ☐ I have a list of the required recurring tasks and recommended frequency to maintain my household members' well-being.
- ☐ I have an efficient and easy to use task tracking system to determine what needs to be done, when it was accomplished, and when it will need to be done again.

30 DAY PROJECT REVIEW QUESTIONS:

1. What does your current task tracking system consist of?
2. What do you like about your current task tracking system?
3. How can your improve your current task tracking system?
4. List the goals you have for this area in your Home Management Notebook.
5. Choose one or two top priority goals from your list to accomplish or get started on this week. Write them in your Home Management Notebook.

Tool Kit:

- ➢ Common Recurring Household Tasks Frequency List (List 4-1)
- ➢ Task Tracker Sheets (Form 4-2)
- ➢ Vehicle Maintenance Record (Form 4-3)
- ➢ Major Appliance List (Form 4-4)
- ➢ Day Planner or Appointment Calendar

SUGGESTIONS FOR FURTHER STUDY:

- ➢ Owner's Manuals for all major appliances and vehicles
- ➢ Manufacturer's internet sites

Day Five
DAILY ROUTINES

"Make it your ambition to lead a quiet life, to mind your own business and to work with your hands, just as we told you, so that your daily life may win the respect of outsiders and so that you will not be dependent on anybody."

1 Thessalonians 4: 11-12 (NIV)

"It's because we have kids," my sister informed me, "they don't have kids so they can keep their homes cleaner."

"Look, those women don't have men who cook," she contemplated, "men are so messy in the kitchen who can keep up with that."

"Not to mention they expect us to work full time and eat so late," I concurred, "that is why we can't keep up."

We comforted our weary souls with one excuse after the other. That worked until I met Julie. Julie had four kids, worked full-time, chauffeured her children to all the latest and greatest events, and did not allow her family to eat at fast food restaurants—she cooked too! Her house was always clean, organized, and inviting. She loved to entertain guests with home made specialties and we all loved to be entertained by her. I wanted to be just like Julie.

No more excuses—I had to figure out how she did it. I learned one thing about Julie—she never rested. She was always on the go and the sad thing was that she never had anytime to just relax and enjoy life. Although she appeared to enjoy things—it became quite evident that she was pretty high-strung and found it difficult to rest. I wanted to figure out a way to have a clean and inviting home. I wanted to be ready for that knock on the door but without losing my joy in life.

My friend Carol, also, had a clean home. She, too, stayed pretty busy but not to the point where she couldn't take a few minutes and enjoy a conversation with friends or just not worry about the tasks on her to do list. What I learned from Carol is that she could break jobs down into small chunks and knock them out one chunk at a time. She could fold a load of clothes on our way out the door to the mall. As she walked through a room, she picked up two or three items and put them where they went. Not less work but more efficient use of energy. Going to the kitchen anyway, take a few dishes with you; heading to the bathroom, take a stack of towels with you.

I had to change my old mindset that cleaning day was a Saturday morning event. In my old mindset laundry night was Thursday night. I hated laundry night and the way my kids went through clothes made laundry night stretch from Thursday evening to consume the whole weekend. I would find any excuse to skip Thursday night but that only led to disaster on Monday morning when the kids had nothing clean to wear to school. Giving up cleaning days and laundry nights meant I needed something other than growing piles of dirty clothes to remind me that these things needed to be done. Although I was a proponent of spontaneity I quickly learned that routines—to my surprise—actually provided me with more opportunity for spontaneous activity rather than limiting it.

In a review of 50 years of research, Dr. Barbara Fiese and her colleagues conclude that predictable family routines promote healthy individuals. Although bad habits can become destructive routines, establishing healthy routines can contribute to positive behavioral, emotional, and physical outcomes. Most childcare centers thrive on routine schedules and transition activities that help children move from one activity to the next. Family routines can also provide children with a sense of security and predictability of daily life. In addition to meal time routines, morning and bedtime routines, and routines at school; establishing cleaning routines can help everyone do a little each day to eliminate the burden of large bulks of cleaning by one person. You will be surprised how even small children can do a little everyday that add up to a bigger job than you would consider asking them to do all at once.

I avoided establishing routines for years because I was afraid I would have to give up my love of being spontaneous. However, routines do not eliminate spontaneity but actually free up more time for adventure and creativity. According to Webster, routines are prescribed courses of actions to be followed regularly. You probably have more routines than you realize but not all of them are adding value to your life. Now is a good time to look at what you want to establish in a day or week and develop a routine to ensure it gets done.

Consider establishing routines in the following areas:

- Personal hygiene
- Morning time
- Bedtime activities
- Family time

- Cleaning Tours
- Mealtime routines
- Homework routines
- Prayer and bible reading
- Checking in with Extended Family

If you can think of other areas you are not accomplishing what you want, those are areas that will benefit from an established routine. Maybe you wanted to write that novel but never have the time. Set aside a fifteen minute block of time each day to work on your novel. By the end of the week not including Sunday, you will have written for an hour and a half. If you do that every week, by the end of the month you will have spent at least six hours writing your novel.

Take twenty minutes a day to complete what we call our cleaning tours, and you have completed two hours of cleaning by the end of the week eliminating the need to be stuck home cleaning on Saturday morning because when you get up Saturday morning the cleaning is done. Cleaning tours include a dish tour, clutter tour, trash tour, and laundry tour. If each time you enter and leave a room you do some zone clean up (see chapter two) , you will have eliminated the bulk of your cleaning tours.

The Daily dishes tour—walk through each room of the house and gather the dishes. This is necessary if you allow kids or have spouses who carry off glasses to their rooms. We also have a glass of water by the bedside and the kids often have drink glasses in the recreation room. So I often send the kids on a dish tour while I start dinner. Gather all the dishes and load them into the dishwasher. If there is room for the evening meal's dishes I leave it, if not I run a load. If you don't have a dishwasher, ask a child to wash up a few dishes as you prepare to cook. If you clean your dishes as you cook, then after the meal you only have your service ware to wash up.

The Daily clutter tour is eliminated by zone clean up. Teach the kids to get in the habit of doing a little zone clean up as they leave and enter each room. Don't forget the rooms you don't use. Since I have my own bathroom, I had forgotten to look at the kids' bathroom which doubled as the guest bathroom. One day when a friend asked to use the restroom I realized it had been awhile since I checked on its condition. The kids had cheerfully accepted the duty to clean it but I hadn't followed up and it was a disaster. "At your own risk," I chuckled and decided from then on to at least use that restroom once a day to evaluate its condition.

Usually the daily laundry tour eliminates most of the clutter in the bathroom. I do this a few minutes after I get home. I ask the kids to bring their laundry baskets to the laundry room when they are half full. I sort them and return the baskets to their rooms with a load of fresh clothes to put away. When I was doing laundry for a family of six, I used to do a load of laundry each day. I started a load when I got home from work, did the other cleaning tours, and then put it in the dryer as we finished dinner. After dinner, I folded and put the clothes away. This eliminated the dreaded laundry night altogether.

The paper tour in our house is probably the biggest clutter eliminator we have. Along with trash that we now burn ourselves, we are inundated with junk mail that the computer age has not entirely eliminated. The need to sort through incoming mail, weeding out the important documents and disposing of the junk mail is a daily process. If you don't keep up, you will be constantly sorting through piles of papers looking for the important documents you are pretty sure you received in the mail. Establish a routine of eliminating the incoming paper trail along with the consumable trash that clutters homes and couch cushions on a daily basis.

When you first start your daily tours—it seems like a lot of work. However, soon you will realize by utilizing your energy efficiently, your labor is less intensive and your house is always clutter-free giving you access and functionality for whatever you need to do: clean, cook, play, relax, or entertain guests. Then you just have to have a plan to quickly and efficiently put the shine on it and you are READY for that knock at the door. Additionally, you will enjoy a home that is clean, organized, functional, and peaceful.

The other routines you establish on a daily basis will help your children and other family members help you more efficiently. Ever notice how family members flock to the cleanest room. They are fresh and inviting.

Now teach them how to help you keep it that way. Their contributions will soon be effortless as they begin to understand your expectations of them and learn the ease and value of their daily contribution.

GETTING STARTED:

Start by listing your daily routine needs such as those listed above. Give each routine a name such as Morning Routine or Daily Cleaning routine. Most routines take between fifteen and thirty minutes. Although something like a mealtime routine may take longer. Use the All Daily Task schedule to list the routines you will complete each day. You may find it helpful to separate your daily task schedule by categories such as work days or weekends. I have four daily routine lists; a Monday-Friday, school day routine list; a Saturday routine list, and a Sunday routine list. On my All Daily Tasks schedule, sample form 5-1, I list the routines along with the time of day I plan to complete them.

For example, Morning Routine is completed Monday-Friday from 5:50am – 6:20am and is listed on the All Daily Tasks sheet for school days. Each task is then listed on the All Daily Task Definition sheet, sample form 5-2, under its corresponding routine name. The Morning routine consists of: Waking up, personal hygiene and getting dressed, waking up the kids, feeding the dogs, checking on the kids personal hygiene routine, letting the horses out, making sure the kids are dressed, setting out breakfast, cleaning up from breakfast, and heading out the door.

As you find routines that help add efficiency to your schedule add them to your routine definitions sheet. Then add the routine name to your All Daily Tasks Schedule I realized that if I unloaded the dishwasher in the morning before I left for work, a 3-minute task, the kids were more likely to put their dirty dishes in the dishwasher instead of the sink and on the counters. This left the counters clear and the kitchen more inviting when I come home from work and need to cook dinner. Eventually the routine becomes habit and you no longer have to look at your definitions or schedule. Review your schedules and definitions whenever you feel like you can't get everything done in a day that you want to accomplish. Prioritize, find out what you can eliminate or become more efficient at, and replace it with the priority things that are being left out.

<circle days> S – M – T – W – R – F – S	Work/School Days Schedule
Times:	Routine:
AM	Dish Tour
PM (after work)	Clothes Tour (start laundry)/Paper Tour/Clutter Tour (zone defense)
5:30pm	Cook/Clean Routine
8pm	Bedtime Routine

Daily Routine Task Schedule and Routine Definitions Sample

Routine Name: Dish Tour							
Tasks to be completed on:	S	M	T	W	R	F	S
Empty Dishwasher of Clean dishes and put away	X	X	X	X	X	X	X
Walk through house and pick up all dishes	X	X	X	X	X	X	X
Return dishes to kitchen and load in dishwasher	X	X	X	X	X	X	X
Clear counters of all dirty dishes and load in dishwasher	X	X	X	X	X	X	X
Start and run dishwasher (Each evening or when full)	X	X	X	X	X	X	X

Since I moved to the ranch, my daily duties have more of an impact. A call from a teacher because you forgot to have your child do his homework is nothing compared to finding your child's pet rabbit died because he forgot to fill its water bottle. To make sure each of the ranch animals are taken care of, my home is always ready for welcoming guests, and I can squeeze in time for completing my favorite projects; I made a list of my daily routine tasks and put it at the front of my day planner. This list can be used with or in place of the All Daily Tasks Schedule. Each of my cleaning tasks take 2 minutes, so I can complete one in the time it takes to heat up a cup of water for my morning tea. There are twelve tasks on my list so that is 24 minutes each day devoted to household cleaning less the 2 minute tasks I delegate to each child. A child is highly more likely to cheerfully accept an assignment to dust the TV stand than he will a command like, "Go clean your room." In addition to 24 minutes worth of cleaning tasks, my list includes 60 minutes of Ranch Chores and 60 minutes of personal routines and projects. Even on a workday that frees up a lot of time. Weekly tasks may either be combined or broken down into smaller tasks. For example, I don't want to spend a whole day doing laundry but if I break down laundry into three daily tasks: gather a load of clothes, wash/dry a load of clothes, and fold/put away a load of clothes then the laundry is always caught up. The house gets routinely dusted if I "dust something" every day.

       Some tasks are combined with similar tasks to maintain a daily habit. Since I don't want to haul out my lawnmower more than once a week I combine that task with my other lawn and garden tasks. In this case, the task line reads "water/weed/mow something." This takes care of the lawn and garden throughout the week. It is considered a 2-minute task during the week when I take a few minutes to pull a couple weeds or water the houseplants. I'll have to allow more time to accomplish the mowing and depending on the season that may be on a weekly or biweekly basis or not at all.

       Choose either the EVERYDAY LIST (see My Every Day List sample) or the Daily Routine Tracker (Form 5-1) and stick with your daily routines for a minimum of 21 days. It takes that long to form a new habit and to really evaluate how your routines are working for you. Whether you use the EVERDAY LIST or the Daily Routine Tracker or a combination of both, you will find that having daily routines will free up time for more adventure without feeling guilty. Your home will be cleaner, more organized, and more ready than ever before.

AFFIRMATIONS:

☐ I have a daily routine that helps me efficiently accomplish the routine tasks that must be done around my home each day and week.

30 DAY PROJECT REVIEW QUESTIONS:

1. What do your current daily routines consist of?
2. What do you like about your current routines?
3. What would you like to change about your current routines?
4. List the goals you have for this area in your Home Management Notebook.

5. Choose one or two top priority goals from your list to accomplish or get started on this week. Write them down in your Home Management Notebook.

TOOL KIT:
- All Daily Tasks Schedule, Form 5-1 and/or My EVERYDAY List (samples)
- All Daily Tasks Routine Definitions Sheet, Form 5-2

SUGGESTIONS FOR FURTHER STUDY:
- *Sink Reflections* by Marla Cilley, www.flylady.net

Day Six
HOUSEHOLD FILES

"This is what the LORD Almighty, the God of Israel, says: Take these documents, both the sealed and unsealed copies of the deed of purchase, and put them in a clay jar so they will last a long time."

Jeremiah 32:14

Do you cringe when your child bounces into your room at bedtime and says, "Oh yea, mom, I have to have a copy of my physical form tomorrow or I can't play basketball." You know you made a copy of the form before you turned it in for soccer camp but now, where is it?

Has your filing system become such a nightmare you are afraid to be in the same room with it? Maybe it consists of neatly sorted categorical piles? You may think neat piles of financial papers, health records, and other sorted projects is an adequate filing system however such a system can prove to be time-consuming and frustrating to find a specific document in. Without a clear system with a sound process for keeping it updated, finding a specific document can be elusive, such as a child's physical form.

After designating my office zone, buying a four-drawer filing cabinet, and stashing all my papers in it; I knew the general area where my documents would be. I still couldn't put my hands on any specific document with the ease and efficiency I desired. So I set up my first system by filing papers in folders with crafty labels and putting them in the filing cabinet never to be found again. Soon I could no longer decipher where to put a folder or how to label it. So I made a 'to be filed' stack. I thought a day would come when I would be more decisive about such matters and I would file them then. Eventually the stacks needed to be put into boxes and the boxes began to pile up in my workspace, eventually they began to take over the entire room, and eventually even claimed spaces in the attic.

I started a few other systems to try to help me out of the mess and to keep track of important projects. It worked for a little while until eventually even those folders were lost in the shuffle. Every time I needed a specific document I had to overhaul my system. Since the label and file routine wasn't working, I knew it was time to develop a system that would work. I tried many resources to find the right system but eventually had to come up with my own. I started with the paper piles around my desk and the unassociated files in my filing cabinet. I thought about how I might use those papers. What are the papers I am constantly searching for? What papers do I use most often? Ask yourself the same questions.

Do you need both an active filing system and a semi-permanent/permanent filing system? Do you prefer to categorize your system chronologically or alphabetically? The system I have developed is a mix of each. It covers most of what you will need as well but may not cover everything. As with any system begin somewhere, stick with it long enough to know its strengths and weaknesses, and then modify it to suit you.

GETTING STARTED:

Set up a room, space, or an area to designate as the Home Office. This is a where the family business will be conducted and important papers and documents stored. The efficiency of this space is of utmost importance but esthetical qualities are what will draw you into the area to perform the more mundane tasks such as filing. Keep this area uncluttered, organized, and enjoyable to be in. Overhaul your current household filing system using a written filing plan.

To set up your filing system, start by copying the filing system index. This is a four drawer system divided into four broad categories: Finances (Current transactions), Assets (Acquired and Maintaining), Home and Family Management, and Archives. Each drawer is then subdivided into categories alphabetically which separate groups of folders according to their categorical topic. The folders in each category can be organized chronologically or alphabetically. For instance, the bill payment records are alphabetical whereas the family health records are filed by individual oldest to youngest.

It is important to have the index prepared before you start, although you may modify it as you go. You will need a four-drawer filing cabinet or four filing boxes, divider cards, labeler or marking pen, and manila folders. Don't worry about the order of the folders in your categorical groups at the beginning. Today, you will just set up your skeleton system by putting the category's topic divider card in each drawer and begin sorting all your papers, folders, and documents into each group behind the appropriate category divider. Then later you can come back to work on organizing each category's folders one at a time.

Begin by labeling each drawer's category card (stiff cardboard filing dividers) as follows according to your personal household needs:

Drawer One- Finances

- Ongoing Transaction Folders
- Bank Accounts
- Bill Payment Records
- Employment Records (current position)
- Estate Plans
- Health Policies (current plan)
- Income
- Insurance
- Investments
- Rental Records (current tenant)
- Tax Receipts (current year)

Drawer Two- Assets

- Contracts and Warranties
- Computer Settings/Security/Recovery & Back up schedule
- Deeds/Titles -- copies--
- Owner/Operator Manuals
- Property Records (Home, Rental Property, Vehicles)

Drawer Three- Home and Family Management

Home Management-

- Contact Information
- Ongoing Project Folders
- Repair Records- Home, Rental Property, Vehicles
- Resource/Referrals
- Zone Maps

Family Records--

- Certificates (Legal)-- copies--
- Education Records
- Health Records
- Pet Records
- Organizations/Memberships
- Wardrobe lists

Genealogical/Family Historical Documents

Drawer Four- Archives
- Past Tax Returns and support documentation
- Past Health Insurance Policies
- Past Employment Records
- Other Archives

Make four copies of the filing system index you are going to use and put one in the front of each filing drawer for easy reference. This document will help you file things correctly and retrieve documents easily.

Next, you can begin putting the dividers into each drawer and sorting your folders and documents into groups behind each category as appropriate. Once you have all your documents at least stashed behind their category card divider you will be well on your way to being organized. At least you will have eliminated most of the piles you normally would have to dig through to find a document.

Each day during your "Paper Tour" you should set aside a few minutes to sort your incoming mail and file your "To File" box. As you do, spend a little extra time sorting out and organizing one of the categories of folders. You will probably find that often you have duplicate folders or folder labels that don't make sense or fit the new system. Order the folders in each category in a way that makes sense for its unique purpose, usually chronologically or alphabetically. You may find it helpful to make an index of the folders in the category group and tape it on the category's divider card. Further organize the papers in each folder as needed.

As you go along purge the files of papers you do not need to keep anymore or those that should be filed in the archives. Here is a short list to help you decide. Consider getting rid of the following:
- Salary statements after checking your W-2 for accuracy. For a record of annual contributions and leave records keep the last one of each year.
- Cancelled checks once they are on the bank statement. Cancelled checks for tax-deductible items can be kept and filed with your tax returns supportive documentation.
- Receipts for non-tax deductible consumables once they are entered in your check book or cash accounting record.

- Expired warranties or owner's manuals for equipment you don't own anymore. Give owner's manuals away with the equipment when you sell it or donate it.
- Expired coupons.
- Information on organizations you no longer belong to. Information from organizations of significant family heritage can be stored with your genealogical files.
- Do not keep memorabilia in this filing system. You can have a separate file for that kept somewhere else like in a craft room/area or near your photo storage.
- The family genealogical file is optional in this location. If you are a family historian and will accumulate a lot of documents, it's best to find a separate location for this information.
- Home business. You should invest in a separate filing cabinet and system for a home business even if you share the same office.

What should you keep then?

- Current and semi-permanent files are kept in the four-drawer system.
- Keep health records indefinitely. This record includes a list of who was visited and when, the diagnosis and treatment. This is invaluable if you ever need to file a disability claim.
- Keep tax returns indefinitely along with the supporting documentation. Keep seven years in your archives drawer. After seven years, put the files in a waterproof filing container in your long-term storage area. It's a good idea if you keep a digital image of your tax records in an offsite location such as at a relative's home or in a safety deposit box.
- Certain legal documents should be kept separately in safe deposit box or fire and moisture- proof safe. These documents are copied and filed in your file system with a list in each folder showing the location of the original document. Instructions for retrieval should be included in your estate plan. Keep a copy of your estate plan in an offsite location such as a relative's home or in a safety deposit box.

Ongoing Transaction Folders are bright, pocket folders that contain all paper work for a pending or ongoing event kept in drawer one. The transaction could be an insurance claim or an erroneous debt you are fighting. Sometimes these activities can go on for years and accumulate a large paper trail. These financial transactions can be managed with ease using the color-coded pocket filing system. When you get a phone call about the project, you can grab the folder and have your entire record in front of you. You can make notes about the phone call on an ongoing log contained in the folder. This is also a great record if you need to make a court appearance. Keep copies of all mail correspondences and phone calls in one place.

Ongoing project folders are similar to the transaction folders. Use brightly, colored pocket folders to keep documents and an ongoing log of phone calls or task lists for an ongoing project. You can keep notes on bidders, or even swatches for a home-improvement project. The idea is that everything is in one place and easily accessible. When the project is complete, you can sort through the paper work and file necessary documents for your records and throw out the rest. I have found that ½" notebooks also work well for larger projects. These are kept on a shelf in the home office next to the filing cabinet. Label the spine so you can quickly retrieve a project notebook.

A CONTINUING PROCESS:

Now that the filing system is set up you need a plan to keep up with it. A filing system is only as good as the process by which it is used and maintained. Start, where the paper trail starts, with incoming mail. Each day during your 'paper tour', sort your mail into five categories: Bills to pay, Action Required, To Be Filed, Read Later, or throw away. I do this while standing very close to a trash can on my way in the door with the mail. I wish I had a trashcan next to my mailbox. As I open the mail, I try to read what I want right away and pitch it immediately if it requires no further action. The 'read laters' I set on the magazine stand to read at my leisure. If I don't read it in a week I pitch it. Magazines and mail order catalogs I use are pitched when the next issue comes. The bills are sorted out into my Bills Payment Ongoing Transactions folder. I open these on payday when I pay my bills. After the bills are paid, I file the paid bills in the appropriate Bill Payment Record folder.

It is important to determine when you will do your filing and when you will do your 'action needed'. More than likely you can write the action necessary on your to do list and file the paperwork in an ongoing folder or other folder. Do this daily and do not let it accumulate. If you have followed these steps, your filing system is set up well enough that you can easily find the appropriate file for a given stack of "To Be Filed" documents in the time it takes you to brush your teeth at night. Put on your favorite song and just do it while you sing along. You will reap the rewards when you need to find that proof of payment or even that copy of your child's most recent physical. Where is it? It's filed under Home and Family Management in the Health Records under that child's name. You got it! Now, go enjoy those basketball games.

AFFIRMATIONS:

- ☐ I have set up a home filing system to keep our families documents in order and easily accessible.
- ☐ I will organize one cluster at a time until the filing system is complete.
- ☐ I will purge and organize the filing system at a regularly scheduled time such as annually. I have annotated this time on my task tracker (see Day Four).
- ☐ I have made copies of our families legal documents and placed the originals in a safety deposit box or fire proof vault. I have filed the copies of these documents appropriately in the home filing system.
- ☐ I have let go of the need to store paperwork that is totally unnecessary eliminating chaos and confusion hindering the retrieval of important documentation for my family.
- ☐ I have placed a copy of my filing system index in the front of each filing drawer so even those unfamiliar with my system can easily find needed documents in my absence.
- ☐ I have set up a system to sort incoming paperwork into five categories: bills, file, action, read, or throw away.
- ☐ I have added time to my All Daily Task schedule to sort mail and file papers so that my family's paperwork will not create chaos in our lives (see Day Five).

30 DAY PROJECT REVIEW QUESTIONS:
1. What does your current household filing system consist of?
2. What is working with your current filing system?
3. How can you improve your current filing system?

4. List the goals you have for this area in your Home Management Notebook.
5. Choose one or two priority goals from you list to accomplish or get started on this week. Write them down in your Home Management Notebook.

TOOL KIT:
- ➢ Four Drawer Filing Cabinet
- ➢ Hard Board Dividers with tabs
- ➢ Manila Folders with tabs
- ➢ Marker or Label Machine
- ➢ Filing System Index (four copies)
- ➢ Clear Plastic waterproof filing tubs (enough for special filing projects such as memorabilia or family genealogy and for tax years older than seven years).
- ➢ Brightly colored pocket folders
- ➢ Time set aside daily to sort mail, file papers, and organize one cluster

SUGGESTIONS FOR FURTHER STUDY:
- *File Solutions: Filing made easy; The Home Filing System* by Don and Nora Donnelly.

Day Seven
PAYING BILLS

"Let no debt remain outstanding, except the continuing debt to love one another, for he who loves his fellowman has fulfilled the law."

Romans 13:8 (NIV)

"You have until July 30th to pay four hundred dollars in back taxes on your townhouse in Douglas County," the notice stated. "If your payment is not received by close of business July 30th the local paper will list your property for sale on Saturday." What? It was July 25th when I received this notice and I had not planned to come up with $400 for taxes this week. I called the county clerk and asked, "Do you usually only give five days notice to pay taxes and then threaten to take the property? What happened to late fees and collection agencies and other such harassment?"

The woman at the county office was very kind. She explained to me that the notice I received was just a courtesy notice before my home was listed in the paper the following Saturday. They didn't have to do that. She said that tax bills come out once a year in November and at that time you choose to pay it all at once or split it into two payments. No other notices are sent out for the second payment. My second payment was due on May 10th and I was already 32 days delinquent. If I had not received the courtesy note, I would have lost my townhouse worth over $80,000 because of a $400 mistake.

The sequence of events occurred because I had paid off my mortgage in February and I was now responsible to pay my own taxes. I had never received a tax bill because the lender had received it in November and they don't send out tax bills for the second payment. She explained that my mortgage company should have told me that the second half was due in

May. I don't recall them telling me that. I was expecting to get a tax bill at some point but expected to have more than 5 days to pay it.

The county doesn't care why the taxes were not paid. My townhouse would have been listed for sale in the paper on August 1st no matter the reason. That is how it is with many of the businesses we owe money to. They don't care that we lost the bill and they probably won't believe you didn't get it at all. Businesses don't care that here in the country, dogs really do eat the mail. To avoid delinquency, late fees, and big losses you need to be aware of when your bills are due and be able to pay them on time whether or not you get the bill in the mail. In addition, knowing what bills you should be expecting and approximately how much they should be will help you budget your spending throughout the month. If you don't receive a bill, you know to call the company and find out how much you owe and when it is due. Often you can get this information online or via automated phone services.

Two forms will help you manage your monthly income wisely and keep a record of where it is going. The first form is the Bill Payment Record. This form also contains your monthly budget categories and how much you will allot to them each time you get paid. Anything in excess of bills paid and set aside for budgeted spending should go into your savings fund. The Bill payment record lists every bill you anticipate receiving, how much you expect it to be and when it is due. The second form is your Savings form. This form is for you to keep track of large purchase needs and savings to pay your annual and semi-annual obligations such as car insurance and property taxes. These two forms are used in addition to your check register and check ledgers that keep track of your accounts and tax deductible spending throughout the year.

GETTING STARTED:

Take a look at the Budget and Bill Paying Record for "Our Ranchero" in appendix Chapter 7 Samples and Forms. Notice I have listed every bill I am aware I will be receiving. I have left blanks at the bottom to write in unexpected bills such as medical co-payments if someone gets sick. Next to the budget category I write the name of the person or company I will be paying. The second half of the row is filled with budgeted areas so that I can allocate my income sources efficiently. The second column is to write the payee number which I use in my online banking. This is becoming more and more popular. The next column is the due date. I usually write this in based on when it was due the previous month. That way I can start checking on an amount if I don't get a bill.

The Status column is used to mark when and how the debt was paid. Occasionally, I may write C/O in the column indicating that I did not pay the bill and have put it on next month's worksheet. The rest of the columns to the right are divided up into sources of money that will be used to pay the bills. I have annotated at the top how often I receive income from these sources and the approximate amounts. The next step is to write in the anticipated amounts of each bill and list it under the income source you expect to use to pay it with. I also include a column on the far right for my annual savings fund which is used to pay certain items. It is called XFER indicating that money will be transferred out of an existing account to pay the items listed below it.

Keep this list in a pocket folder. Label one pocket "To Pay" and the other "To File." When a new bill comes in the mail, put it immediately in the To Pay pocket. Sit down once a week with each new bill, cross through the estimated amount due and write in the exact amount due and it's exact due date. If you will be writing a check, annotate on the bill that you have written the amount and dates on your worksheet and leave the bill in the "To Pay" pocket. If you pay online or through a payment service you can place the bill in the "To File" pocket. Do this for all bills you have received.

If you use the three pocket folder, which I recommend, label them "Incoming Bills", "To Pay," and "To File." Place incoming bills in the incoming pocket immediately as you sort through your day's mail. When you have annotated the amounts on your bill payment worksheet, transfer the bill to the "To pay." On each payday sit down, pay your bills either by check, payment service, or online and annotate your record form and/or bill that it has been paid, how much, the date, and by what method (include confirmation numbers or check numbers) and put the bill in the "To File" pocket. No less than once a week, take the papers out of the 'To File" pocket and place them in your home filing system.

Use the given categories on the blank Bill Payment Record (Form 7-1) to write in the names of the companies you pay each month. Use your current system to recall as many as you can and write in the rest as the bills come in. Draw a line underneath the recurring bills listed on your form and begin writing in your budget categories from the possible budget categories list. For the first few months use a pencil until you have a good idea what kind of budget is working for you. After you pay your tithes, remember to pay your Savings account out of every source of income you receive. You'll use these funds to pay annual bills and obligations as well as build a cushion for unexpected expenses. Remember one thing: you can expect unexpected expenses, you just can't anticipate when or how much they will be.

Use the columns on the right to write in your anticipated incomes and list your anticipated bill amounts under a column of income that meets that need either because of the amount of the bill or the date it is due. Remember to allow time for mailing and posting as you figure out when you want to pay the bill. For larger bills that require funds from more than one source, use two rows. The first row is savings to pay the bill and the second row is the payment or transfer from savings to pay the debt. For example, it takes me two pay periods to save enough to pay my mortgage. So on one line I write, "Savings to pay my mortgage." I divide the total payment in two and put a figure in each column. When I pay my bills for that income date I transfer that amount to savings. When it is time to pay the bill, I transfer the money back out, pay the bill, and annotate the payment on the row that says Mortgage company payment and write the amount under the column Transferred from Savings. Don't be afraid to pay bills early. Even if you take money from an interest bearing account, you will save money by avoiding late fees and often posting early will save you in interest from that point on.

Keep your bill payment worksheet in the pocket folder with your incoming bills. Although a two pocket folder works fine, I have a really nice four pocket vinyl folder that I use. I label my pockets: "Incoming bills" "To Pay" "To File" and "Schedule/Payment Record." I also keep a list from my bank with all my payee numbers and addresses/account numbers of those not on my payee list. The Bill Payment Record is stored in the top drawer of my filing cabinet for easy access.

Once you have paid your bills you will need a system for filing them. I staple all the notices from one company together with the most current on top and keep them in a cluster according to category type. They are filed in Drawer One of the filing cabinet (see Day 6) under the subdivision titled Bill Payment Records. For example, all credit card bills are kept together in the consumer credit folder and each credit card notice is stapled on top of the previous months' notice. If I need a history of my payments on the credit card, I grab the stapled stack and have all the notices for that year together. Another folder is set up for Utilities; the water bills, electric bills, and gas bills are kept in that folder. I clean out each folder annually when I do my taxes.

The second form that is helpful in stewardship of your money is a savings form. I list all my accounts on this form and their intended uses. For instance, I have a Money Market account set aside for my Emergency Fund. When I can I transfer money into the account and I do not touch anything in that account unless it meets the pre-established requirements I developed for what constitutes an emergency. The goal of this account is to provide the equivalence of three months of my current income should I not be able to work. I have figured out what three months of income is and set that as my goal for this account. I have a good start on the account but definitely not three months of income. It also earns the best interest of my cash accounts so it helps keep up with inflation as well as slowly push me towards my goal.

I have another money market account set up for my annual savings fund (ASF). It earns a good interest rate but only allows a few withdrawals a month. I have a regular allotment that goes into this account that is equal to my anticipated annual obligations divided by the number of pay days contributing to the account. We also have a checking and savings account set up for our regular checking and bill paying. I also budget an amount for savings to the ASF for large purchases. The Savings form includes columns for listing goals, anticipated needs, and prioritizing savings incentives such as a new truck or cash for home improvements. If you begin to treat your savings like a bill obligation, soon you will be using your own money to make your major purchases—even cars--- and the freedom of being out of debt will allow you to save even more. For example, if you put off that major auto purchase for three years and make the payment you think you can afford to yourself instead of the bank, in three years you can buy two cars.

If you are not sure where your money is disappearing each month you may need to create a FACE IT log. Face where your money goes each month by keeping an on-going log of where you spend your money. Save all your receipts each month. Get a receipt or make one each time you spend cash. Save all your debit and credit receipts. Clean out your pockets and purse every night like you would spare change, dropping your receipts into a small box or folder each day. Each month total your receipts into each designated category on an accounting ledger. This is a good time to split out receipts for tax purposes. Put receipts for assets in the appropriate file (I usually staple them to the inside of the folder where I keep the item's owner's manual.) and keep a general purchases receipts folder for items that may need to be returned such as clothes or gifts. Once you have entered

the amounts in your monthly FACE IT log, filed your tax receipts, asset receipts, and return receipts, you can shred the rest of the receipts. You don't
need to keep receipts for non-tax deductible fast food or bank receipts that
have already appeared on your monthly statement. Total your ledger columns each month and in a few months (a minimum of three) you can calcu-
late an average in each category and adjust your spending habits accordingly.

To be a good steward of your money you need to know what you
have coming in, what you have going out, who and what you owe, and be
prudent about paying your debts in a timely fashion. If you are having trouble with your finances, seek a godly advisor. Don't forget to keep track of
your assets as well (Day 9), you might be able to use them to increase your
income or pay off your consumer debt. The goal is to use only what we have
been given, use it generously and efficiently, and to let what we have produce more.

AFFIRMATIONS:
- ☐ I have a written schedule of bills due and a plan to pay them even if the bill is displaced.
- ☐ I have put my bill paying and check reconciling tasks on my task tracker.
- ☐ I have a written spending budget and savings plan.
- ☐ I know what money I have coming in, how I spend it, who and what I owe, and am paying off my debts in a timely fashion.

30 DAY PROJECT REVIEW QUESTIONS:
1. What does your current bill paying system consist of?
2. What about your current bill paying system works well?
3. What about your current bill paying system needs improvement?
4. List the goals you have for this area in your Home Management Notebook.
5. Choose one or two priority goals from your list to accomplish or get started on this week. Write them down in your Home Man-agement Notebook.

TOOL KIT:
- ➢ Bill Payment Record (Form 7-1)
- ➢ Budget Category possibilities list (Form 7-2)
- ➢ Savings Allocations Form (Form 7-3)
- ➢ Face it log (Form 7-4)

SUGGESTIONS FOR FURTHER STUDY:

- ➢ *Financial Peace* by Dave Ramsey
- ➢ *Total Money Makeover* by Dave Ramsey
- ➢ *Money Matters* by Larry Burkett

Day Eight
PERSONAL CARE

"Do you not know that in a race all the runners run, but only one gets the prize? Run in such a way as to get the prize."

1 Corinthians 9:24 (NIV)

When the question, "What's for dinner?" became "Where are we eating dinner?," I knew it was time to review our dinner routine. Had we really been eating out that much? I have to admit driving through a fast food lane is an attractive alternative to going home after a 10-hour shift and cooking a meal for the family. Not to mention the ease of using a debit card and bringing home individually wrapped portions to divvy up at the kitchen table. Drive-through meals that are personalized to each family member also increase consumption. No more picky eaters to turn down that meal you barely found the energy to put together.

I don't mind cooking but I do mind a few things that go along with it, such as, having someone complain about what you have prepared or not having the correct items on hand to make the meal. The shopping and the planning and the refusal to eat certain things, like no onions, no sauce, and no peppers, can be disheartening. So to get the meal out of the way and move on to the things I enjoy doing with my family, I had started a habit of driving through on the way home from work and having the evening meal over with.

There are a lot of reports in the media that fast food was causing Americans to be obese. It made me reevaluate how often we were eating out. However, I noticed that my family was not becoming obese and I started paying a little more attention. Why not? Even when we ate out four to seven days a week we were not putting on weight. Then one evening, I was taking my son and a friend of his who struggled with his weight out the ranch where we kept our horses. We drove through a fast food lane to grab something to eat and his friend tried to order a double quarter-pounder and a 44-ounce soda. I told him "Sorry, we have rules. Rule number one is that you may only order one regular sandwich or two small sandwiches, a small side, and a medium drink maximum." It made me wonder, "Is the problem with obesity portion control?"

Does portion control keep us thinner even though we eat out as much as the average American family or more? My mother had always taught us the simple rule, "Everything in moderation." I think when it comes to food and dieting and staying in good health it is the small things we do that add up. Smaller portions, a little more exercise, a little less snacking than the average bear and it all adds up to carrying a few less pounds. In our case, we limited our portions and stayed active at the ranch two to three times a week. But there were still things I knew we could change to improve our health.

My biggest hang up was soda pop. I got into the habit of picking one 32-ounce fountain drink up on my way to work and another 32-ounce fountain drink on my way home. Soon it was apparent that I was putting on some weight. The day I felt I had to run to the Quick Shop and get a soda even on my day off, I realized that I was starting to depend on the caffeine and the sugar to get me moving in the morning. I didn't just need a soda to get me going it had to be a fountain soda from the best fountain mixes in town. I decided I did not want to be controlled by that desire so I fastest from all soda for three days. After three days, I no longer craved it and stopped thinking about it constantly. I decided I would only drink a fountain drink when we dined out on special occasions. For awhile that worked great, but then eventually I found myself justifying the need to eat out so that I could have my fountain drink. I realized what I really needed to do is change my drink altogether. I decided to change my drink of choice to ice tea without sugar.

To make it fun and exciting I bought a bag of real lemons to slice and put in my glass. I put the glasses in the freezer to frost them. I still missed a sweet drink now and then so I decided to learn to make real lemonade. We made ice cubes from lemonade to make the drink more fun. The ice cubes melt into a slushy form and make a tasty treat at the end of your drink. I kept adding interesting drinks and refreshments to my arsenal. I became equipped to end my dependence on soda. I lost about 15 pounds as a bonus, something I was totally not expecting.

When my twenty-year old son went to join the military they told him he had to lose ten pounds in order to pass his physical. He was very concerned about that because most people don't have much success on diets. I told him to pick one thing that was his worst dietary habit and eliminate it by replacing it with something fun—like real lemons in the ice tea. He told me that he was drinking almost a half case of canned soda a day. I warned him about diet pop. Switching to diet pop, is not a life changing habit. It is just disguising a bad habit. An eight-year University of Austin Texas study showed that people who drank diet pop gained more weight than people who drank regular pop. They believe it is due to the fact that the palate fools the body into thinking it is going to get a lot of calories but then when doesn't it increases its appetite to make up for the calories it didn't get.

My son decided to change to natural spring water which he enjoyed cold from the fridge. He put a twist of fresh squeezed fruit in it occasionally to add some flavor to his palate. The first two weeks he had lost the 10 pounds and was working on losing four more just to give himself a cushion. His bonus reward was that his acne began to clear up and his complexion began to reflect the changes he had made for his health.

GETTING STARTED:

It is the small steps of REAL CHANGE that make the biggest impact on our health. By small I mean, concentrate on one thing at a time and make that a real habit change. Some are harder than others. If you know the worst habit you have right now is smoking, and if you've tried to stop you know, it's not going to seem small even though it's only one habit. And I won't begin to advise you how to stop smoking. But I will share with you some insight on habit changing.

#1 Focus on the replacement behavior, not the behavior you are giving up. Focus your attention on making your new behavior appealing and enjoyable—like the lemonade ice cubes in the lemonade. Whenever you think of picking up the old habit, reach for the new appealing and enjoyable replacement behavior. The replacement behavior should eliminate the need for the old behavior. Such as drinking the lemonade, eliminates the desire for pop by quenching your thirst and satisfying the palate.

In addition, concentrate on the benefits of making the healthier choice as you make your decision. When I quit smoking, I concentrated on my dream of becoming a singer. If I got a craving for a cigarette, I did breathing exercises and practiced singing until the craving quit.

#2 Plan to continue the new habit at least 21 days before you modify it. Then you will know if it is working or not. Use the 21 Day Habit Tracker to check off each day you were successful.

#3 Plan an incentive for yourself. Choose a small reward to look forward to after you have successfully replaced the old behavior with the new one for 21 days. Circle the days you are successful and draw an X over the days you are not. Consider it practice for the real thing. After 21 days count up your successes, reward yourself for trying and start again. Attempt again to continue the new habit successfully for 21 days, increasing the number of successful days each time, until you have successfully replaced the old behavior with the new behavior for 21 days in a row.

#4 Repeat the 21 day cycles until the old behavior is history. Each time through a 21 day cycle should get easier. By the time you have successfully repeated the 21-day cycle one to three times around, you will have established a new habit in place of the old one. Congratulations!

In addition to changing bad habits, it is important to develop a daily routine of good habits. As a busy mom or career woman or both, you may think you are doing a service to others by rushing your self-care routines but that just leads to burnout and increases your risk of poor health. Allow enough time each day to relax alone and store up energy. Refresh yourself by soaking in the bath or singing in the shower. Start your day with a mini-spa, a hot towel over your face. Then put on a touch of makeup even if you don't plan to leave the house. If you are cramped for time, take another look at your to-do list. Cross the least pressing thing off your list so you will have time to pamper yourself, just a little, every day. Add a personal care time routine to your daily tasks list. Don't forget to include things like hair cuts on your task tracker.

Many people think they don't have time to exercise, but I say, you don't have time to not exercise. Convicted to commit to three cardio-interval workouts a week when Denise Austin announced she was 45 not 28, I have felt better than ever. At 45 I made my commitment to exercise at least three times a week and I noticed the difference after the first week. After the second week, I realized I was much more efficient at everything I did. I had more energy and thus more time left over after my chores were done. I had well made up the 20 minutes I committed to work out in the difference it made in the efficiency of my other activities when I didn't drag through them. Use the habit calendar and cross off the days you do at least 20 minutes of cardiovascular activity. The check off is good motivation and a great tracker. You can see at a glance how your fitness program is working out.

To ensure you stay alert and increase your cumulative workout potential, take mini-stretch breaks and toning breaks all day long. You can do leg-lifts at your desk and stretches in the bathroom cubicle. Take the stairs up and down a few times during your morning break. Sit on an exercise ball while you watch your favorite show—balancing works your leg muscles and your tummy muscles and usually springs you into action to work out during the commercials. Put on a praise and worship CD and complete a 20 minute aerobic dance routine. You can learn the routines off a workout DVD and then complete them to a 20 minute CD of your choice.

Don't wait until you join a gym to start your workout routine. Start today. You can do everything you need right now at home. If you still want to join the gym, that is fine, but have your regular home routine in place and just use the gym to add variety to your routine. Your home gym can be very simple: A DVD workout tape, a few light weights, an exercise ball, a small mat or towel, and your body weight. You can even do body presses on the bathroom wall at work, deep knee bends next to the filing cabinet, or leg lifts sitting at your desk. Remember it all adds up—twenty short routines only one minute long throughout the day add up to a twenty minute routine recommended four times a week for your health.

Good nutrition, eating at home, and a regular workout routine will go along way in making you fit for service to your family and more productive at any of your endeavors. Watching my grandfather grow old, he lived to be 105 years old, I saw him slowly loose the ability to see, to hear, and eventually to walk. I learned by watching him that it isn't as important to stay healthy to live a long life but it is important to stay fit to enjoy life as long as we live.

AFFIRMATIONS:

- ☐ I have chosen a new behavior to replace an unhealthy habit and started tracking my success with the 21-Day Tracker.
- ☐ I have chosen a fitness routine and am monitoring my success with a habits calendar.
- ☐ I have put my personal care routine on my daily task list.

30 DAY PROJECT REVIEW QUESTIONS:

1. What does your current personal care and fitness routine consist of?
2. What is beneficial about your current personal care and fitness routine?
3. What about your current personal care and fitness routine needs improvement?
4. List the personal care and fitness habits you would like to change in your Home Management Notebook.
5. Choose one or two priority behaviors you would like to change and their replacement behaviors or choose one or two priority goals in this area to accomplish or get started on this week. Write them in your Home Management Notebook.
6. Complete a task tracker for each new behavior and a habit calendar for each new habit.

TOOL KIT:

- ➤ Habits Calendar, Form 8-1
- ➤ 21 Day Habits Tracker, Form 8-2

SUGGESTIONS FOR FURTHER STUDY:

- *The Creation Health Breakthrough: 8 Essentials to Revolutionize Your Health Physically, Mentally, and Spiritually* by Monica Reed and Donna K. Wallace

Day Nine
ESTATE PLANNING

"A good man leaves an inheritance for his children's children."

Proverbs 13:22 (NIV)

We were in the emergency room again, ten years after my husband was diagnosed with terminal cancer. I had been here before, left in the waiting room while doctors assessed his situation wondering, "Is this really it?" Never before had the attendant asked the dreaded question, "Does your husband have a living will?" We had thought about preparing one but no he didn't have one. I turned to my friend and asked, "Why is he asking me that?"

"It's a standard question," the attendant said.

"No, it isn't." I insisted. "I have been to the emergency many times over the last ten years and I have never been asked that question."

The next evening my husband died. Even though we had known for ten years it was a possibility, we never expected it, at least not that day. We had no living will, we had no will, we had no estate plans, we had no idea it was time. My husband may have had a better idea than me but he didn't want to talk about it. Dying is difficult to discuss for many of us and so planning for arrangements in the event of our death is often neglected and put off until after we die. For my husband, talking about these things was admitting defeat in his battle with terminal cancer. Becoming a single parent without any advanced planning made me realize, I didn't want my kids to have to handle all the details in their time of grief and most of all, I didn't want the government making plans for my kids.

However, estate planning is not limited to single parents because having the burden of the entire household unexpectedly thrown into your lap when half of a couple dies can be pretty overwhelming and financially disastrous. Often in a couple's situation, the house runs smoothly because

one of the partners handles certain management items such as the finances. Unfortunately as long as things appear to be running smoothly the other
partner is often unaware of the true state of the household's finances. An
estate plan can help keep you or your family from being financially uproot-
ed in the event of the death or inability of the financial manager to function
in that role.

The estate plan, whether you are single or married, poor or rich, will
help you evaluate what might happen if you died today or tomorrow and
help you plan an easier transition for those left behind. It's also a good way
to prepare a contingency plan if you become ill or disabled. Anyone over the
age of twenty-one should have an estate plan prepared and review it periodically. Estate plans should be reviewed after a major life event such as a
marriage, the birth of a child, a divorce, or the death of a loved one.

Other financial planning that should be considered includes emergency planning and retirement savings. How will you carry on financially if
you or your spouse becomes disabled? Most experts advise having at least
three months expenses available in a cash account. Can you maintain your
current or desired lifestyle in your retirement? What about increasing medical needs in your golden years?

GETTING STARTED:

This chapter is not a substitute for legal advice but rather an over-
view of items you should consider in your household management plan.
Having these documents thought through before you visit your lawyer will
help you save time and money. Having given thought to the items listed,
you will be able to answer many of the questions your attorney will be asking as you prepare the legal side of your estate plan.

I have compiled a list of the items most experts agree you should
have in your estate plan along with some of the definitions from Jean
Chatzky's book, *You don't have to be Rich*. Consider each item and complete
all that apply. Have an attorney review your plan as you go along.

Estate Plan Items:
1) <u>An emergency information contact sheet.</u> List the names and contact
   information of your closest family members, trusted neighbors, doctors,
   lawyers, clergyman, accountant, and the executor of your estate. Do not
   list the location of your will but make sure there are at least two people
   on this list that know where it is. Your complete estate plan will be lo-

cated in a safe place and should only be available to your most trusted executives and your attorney.

Since I also run a ranch, I keep my ranch emergency contacts on this sheet as well including the name and number of my vet and ranch helpers that are aware of the needs of the ranch in my absence. Several of my closest friends are aware of my household management notebook which contains valuable information to run my home if I am laid up or out of the country. These extra contacts are vital if you are a sole proprietor running a small business or leasing property.

2) A durable power of attorney. This gives another person the right to manage your finances, both tax and legal matters, if you are sick, disabled, or out of the country.
3) A living will and a health care proxy. The living will pertains to life support in a hospital setting. The health care proxy allows another individual to make health-related decisions on your behalf.
4) A will. The will is your wishes for property allocation upon your death.
5) Life Insurance. This can help your beneficiaries pay for funeral expenses, final bills and debt. In addition it's a good idea to carry enough insurance to help your spouse or children maintain their current lifestyle while they adjust to your absence.
6) Beneficiaries. In your estate plan, you should include the list of beneficiaries for your asset accounts such as checking accounts, savings, and life insurance policies. You can also list these in your will but some accounts such a 401K will not recognize a will and will allocate assets in accordance with your last beneficiary statement on file or in the absence of a statement the laws of the state. How will your beneficiaries know who they are and how to claim their benefits? Answer these questions in your plan.
7) Executors: These are the people you have named to ensure the estate is distributed and carried out as you wished.
8) Trusts. Property held by one party for another until conditions are met.
9) Business interests Value of personal shares, debt, value and care of crops and livestock
10) Estate, gift, inheritance taxes: Taxes on the transfer of property
11) Transfer of dependent care: Naming a Legal Guardian of minors.
12) Personal Interests Accounts receivable, charities, final arrangements

13) <u>Debts</u> Keeping an up to date list of your debts can help family members avoid fraudulent debt in your absence by tracking accounts and closing accounts when necessary.
14) <u>Retirement Plans</u>
    a) IRA's
    b) 401K
    c) Social Security
    d) Employer Retirement Plans
    e) Savings/Securities
    f) Mortgages paid off/debt paid off
15) <u>Other Insurance Policies</u>
    a) Health
    b) Home
    c) Vehicles
16) <u>Other Accounts</u>
    a) Bank accounts—checking, savings, money markets, CD's
    b) Beneficiary forms
    c) Other Benefit accounts
    d) Online accounts and digital assets such as Internet sites.
17) <u>Assets</u>
    a) Inventory
    b) Titles and Deeds
    c) Income Sources

An estate plan is usually what spells out your wishes for the transfer of your wealth, from investments to your favorite slippers. Your legal estate also includes what you owe others including your credit card debt, mortgages, personal IOU's, and taxes. Your will or Last Will and Testament, spells out your goals for all assets as well as those living beings under your care. If no legal guardian survives, the state will otherwise appoint one. Whether you are a single parent or a couple, you should think about who would rear your children, take care of your beloved pets, or tend to your crops and livestock should you or the both of you not be able to.

Though there is quite a bit involved in setting up an estate plan, it isn't as hard as it looks. Trying to narrow down all the possibilities for your particular situation would be impossible to do in one small chapter of this book. My intention is to get you thinking, to get you to review what you already have, and to get you to take the next step to improve your current plan. Get something in writing and get it into the hands of those necessary to make it a legal reality if something happened to you tomorrow. If you aren't sure where to begin, I suggest purchasing Jordan Simon and Brian Caverly's book, *Estate Planning for Dummies.* In that book you can pick and choose the particulars that apply to you.

Draw out a rough plan before you seek an attorney so you can answer the questions they are going to ask you. There is also software available to use to see what the questions are. When you have a good idea what you want to see happen, then hire an attorney to finalize it and make sure it can legally happen as you set forth.

Get something in writing today because death happens and can catch us by surprise. Even though we all know death is inevitable, hoping it won't be today can not replace the peace of being prepared. You have worked hard to accumulate the assets you have so take the extra time to make sure they transfer according to your wishes. You'll be surprised there is more to it than just splitting your assets between the surviving children. Without your involvement, they will have a hard time even knowing what you have to split and arguments over assets can sever their relationships.

Another good book for setting up an inheritance for your kids is "Splitting Heirs" by Ron Blue. If you have a lot of assets to transfer, this book addresses how to make sure your kids can manage their inheritance without becoming dependent on it and running it out too quickly. It makes your inheritance work for them and those you wish to support with your hard earned assets.

Your estate plan is more than just the transfer of control over your assets after you die. It also includes the running of your estate should you become ill or disabled. This is an important factor that people often forget about. The estate plan can help you continue to run your household while you are incapacitated and keep you from losing it if you are unable to work. A good plan will also protect your assets and standard of living should you not be able to return to work.

AFFIRMATIONS:

- ☐ I have a completed an estate plan and at least one other person knows where to find it upon my death or if I become unable to manage my own affairs.

☐ My estate plan is a comprehensive plan that accounts for multiple scenarios including temporary and permanent disabilities as well as death.

30 DAY PROJECT REVIEW QUESTIONS:

1. What does your current estate and financial plan consist of?
2. What about your current plan is working?
3. What about your current plan needs improvement?
4. List the goals you have for your estate and financial plans in your Home Management Notebook.
5. Choose one or two priority goals to accomplish or get started on today. Write them in your Home Management Notebook.

TOOL KIT:

➤ Emergency contact list in your Home Management Notebook.
➤ A completed and comprehensive Estate Plan updated annually or after a major life transition.
➤ A thorough Financial Plan updated after major life transitions.
➤ A durable power of attorney and declared executive of your estate.

SUGGESTIONS FOR STUDY:

➤ *You Don't Have to Be Rich* by Jean Chatzky
➤ *Splitting Heirs* by Ron Blue
➤ *Estate Planning for Dummies* by Jordan Simon and Brian Caverly

Day Ten
SPIRITUAL NUTRITION

Jesus answered, "It is written: 'Man does not live on bread alone, but on every word that comes from the mouth of God."

Matthew 4:4

"I barely get time to read a little scripture each week well enough complete a read-the-bible-in-a-year plan," Jean explained when I shared with her the topic of my daily reading. "I get up at 5:00am, have a quick cup of coffee, get ready and head to work. I leave work around 6:00pm, get back home around 7:00pm, have dinner, go to bed, and get up and do it all over again."

"Through wisdom we gain prudence, knowledge, discretion, counsel, judgment, understanding, and power." I shared with excitement. "I got that little treasure from today's reading alone."

"Wow!" Jean responded.

"Wisdom teaches us to hate evil, pride, arrogance, evil behavior, and perverse speech. If you seek wisdom, the word promises you will find it along with its enduring wealth and prosperity, a full treasury, life, and favor from the Lord. Therefore, delight in wisdom day after day. That beats a do-nut on your way to work."

"I don't have time to eat a donut." Jean said.

"I got all that from one short chapter in Proverbs 19. Surely you could find a moment to read one chapter from a book of the bible. Can you get up five minutes earlier or read while you are drinking that first cup of coffee?"

After talking with Jean she decided to take her bible to work and read a chapter on her first break. That left lunch and afternoon break to continue to socialize with her co-workers. I like that; God first then friends.

My friend, Holly, and I were just discussing how we always set up our daily bible reading plan but then find excuses to let the habit slip until we find ourselves in despair and feeling far from God. "Well, I wouldn't want to be 'religious,'" I often thought. Although reading God's word should be something we do cheerfully, I soon realized that the whole "don't be religious about it" excuse is a trick Satan uses to deceive us. He knows we are made stronger when we read God's Word regularly. Advice in scripture has the power to turn the outcome of the situations we encounter from disaster to delight.

Today's reading from Proverbs says that it is in the word where we find Wisdom and Wisdom is where we find life and favor in the Lord. Isn't that exciting! It is through his word he gives us a full treasury, enduring wealth and prosperity. We are instructed to delight in His wisdom day after day not laboriously read the words each day. It is best if we try to keep it as simple as telling a child good morning each day. Even if you feel a little grumpy, you will leave joyfully.

Before I read, I pray for wisdom. I am always delighted to receive some treasure in my reading which makes me want to come back for more. If I have time I may continue reading and often read another chapter in the evening before bed. At times I like to savor the flavor of a short chapter, taking more time to ponder the parts that touch my heart and life. My daily reading has become too important and joyful to miss!

There are many treasures for us in God's word. I love Galatians and as a matter of fact, Galatians 5:22 was the first thing God revealed to me when I was saved. The fruit of the Spirit-- love, joy, peace, patience, kindness, goodness, faithfulness, gentleness, and self-control. Against such things there is no law. I remember thinking, "Wow! If I had all nine of those in my life-- what else would I need?" I shared that with my first bible study group like a young child talking about a cherished Christmas gift. They smiled and shook their heads. At the time I didn't realize it was a very popular verse printed on cups, plates, hats, and t-shirts available at Christian bookstores everywhere.

Galatians 5 also teaches us that "It is for freedom Christ has set us free." Do we really know what that means for our lives. Are we living out that freedom in our daily lives? Why do we get so wrapped up in the do's and don'ts of being Christian and following Christ? In Malachi 2: 2 I read "... set your heart to honor my name." It isn't a matter of whether we should or shouldn't, it's a matter of getting our heart right and reaping the blessings of that. I think this is what God was trying to teach us through Cain and Abel and their offerings. One is given with joy and the other out of duty. Do you come to the word of God out of duty saying, 'Got to do my daily reading, Check that off?' Or do you come because you are anticipating the JOY God has for you in the application of his word in your life?

"I can't wait to sit down and see what God has for me today!" It's like eating a breakfast you know is good for you-- it tastes good and you know it is going to build up something in you that you will be able to use all day long. "We eagerly [by faith] await through the Spirit the righteousness for which we hope." In Ephesians we are taught that the sword of the spirit is the word of God; a weapon we need in our arsenal. Our daily time in the word is often called our Daily Bread. It is the bread of life, our spiritual nutrition.

GETTING STARTED:

The first thing you need is a bible. I bought my first bible at a garage sale for 25 cents. Then develop a flexible but regular reading plan. I decided to read the bible in a year and got a plan from our church. I continued to fail to keep on that schedule so I decided to just check off on the plan what I did read and watch my progress.

If you would like to keep track of the parts of the bible you have read that is a good way to do it. Type "Bible Reading Plan" in your online search engine and you'll find many options to download, print, or have daily reading plans emailed to you. As you read, you can check off the chapters you read and keep track of your progress through the bible. Try not to stress about how much you read each day but instead concentrate on developing a daily habit of spending some quiet time with the Lord in His word.

Although it is good to read through the entire bible, checking off every chapter in the bible is not the goal. The goal is to feed on God's word daily for your own spiritual nutrition. Allow God to lead you to the areas you should read but if you don't feel a prompting just use your plan to see where to go next. Don't try to read so much that you get nothing out of the reading. Take smaller bites and chew on them longer.

Keeping a written journal of notes from your daily readings is a wonderful way to record specific insights from God's word as you receive them. I often write down questions I am seeking guidance for and then any answers I receive for them as I read. I also write down little treasures from the word that I fall in love with. The following exercises are ideas that can help you savor the flavor of the word– do one or more of them as you read.

Bible Reading Exercises:

- ❑ Make a To Do list from the passages you are reading.
- ❑ List the characteristics of God you learn about in your reading.
- ❑ List God's promises spelled out in your reading.
- ❑ Choose a verse from your reading and write it out on an index card. Carry it with you and peak at it throughout the day.
- ❑ Make a list of direct quotes from Jesus.
- ❑ Choose a passage and look up all the reference passages associated with it.
- ❑ Choose a verse from your reading and pray through it.
- ❑ Choose a passage and teach it to your kids or share it with a friend.
- ❑ Choose one or two passages from your reading and break them down into smaller pieces and meditate on each part.

Find a quiet place and time you can enjoy reading and meditating on God's word. Make it a daily appointment and put it on your daily task list. I used to get up a few minutes early before work and read the word with a cup of tea. However, once school was back in session I found that to be too hectic. So I opted for Jean's idea, spending my first break at work nibbling on the word. It is such a habit now that I feel like I didn't get a break if I miss it. At the end of the day before we read anything else, the boys and I often re-read together whatever section I felt led to read in the morning. It never fails to speak into their lives as well. On the weekends I still enjoy my first cup of tea with my morning bible reading.

My friend, Carol, told me she just couldn't remember to bring her bible to work everyday. She decided to read a chapter in the evening as she winds down on her deck after dinner. It reminded me of a passage I read enjoying a sunset on my father-in-law's deck, "Where morning dawns and evening fades, you call forth songs of joy," Psalm 65: 8. What a great idea! Who wants to miss a song of joy from God? I love being in God's word while watching the sun rise and the sun set from the deck. It's as if the angels are singing and Joy is being sewn into my heart.

God's word is nourishment to our souls without which we will wither away. The sword of the spirit is the word of God. It is what we rely on in times of trouble and in walking out God's will for our lives. We need to know what it says as well. Develop a daily bible reading schedule and stick with it. As you read and meditate on the scriptures, allow God to transform your heart and soul and mind. Apply what He shows you to your daily life.

AFFIRMATIONS:
- ☐ I have set aside a time and place to read God's word daily.
- ☐ I have a journal to record the treasures God shares with me through his word.

30 DAY PROJECT REVIEW QUESTIONS:
1. What is your current bible reading plan?
2. What about your daily bible reading plan is working?
3. What about your daily bible reading plan needs improvement?
4. List the goals you have for this area in your Home Management Notebook.
5. Choose one or two priority goals from this area you can accomplish or get started on today. Write them in your Home Management Notebook.

TOOLKIT:
- ➢ Bible Reading Plan
- ➢ Bible Reading Journal
- ➢ Quiet Place and Time

SUGGESTIONS FOR FURTHER STUDY:
- ➢ *The One Year Bible* by Tyndale House Publishers, Inc.

Day Eleven
HOUSE RULES

"Whoever practices and teaches these commands will be called great in the kingdom of heaven."

Matthew 5:17

Having three kids can be a little tricky. We had our first three children two years apart so at one point we had run out of arms with very mobile two, four, and six year olds. Even with both parents present we lost the six-year-old in a Super Wal-Mart because he didn't wander around the corner of the next aisle when the rest of us did. He looked up and we were gone. It was a new Wal-Mart and there were helpers on roller skates talking on handheld radios trying to locate him. It was very scary.

In his six-year-old mind, he decided that since we had left him he would just wander on over to the video games he had seen as we came in the store. We found him, after our frantic search, happily pretending to play the demo games. Most parents of two or more children can recount more than one story of a child disappearing. In days of rampant abductions and amber alerts, it can be extremely frightening not knowing where your child is. Parenting certainly gets more challenging as the number of children increases and soon you feel like you have lost control.

Now that my kids are older we have a running joke in the family, "Who ate the Cottage Cheese?" but at the time the phrase was coined it was quite frustrating. To this day no one has admitted to eating the entire quart of cottage cheese and putting the empty container back in the refrigerator. Someone got away with lying about the cottage cheese and then things escalated from there. The kids started stealing from one another and taking things from our bedroom. With four little suspects, it was difficult to determine who did it. I would line the kids up, a little trick I learned from my dad, and try to get one of them to break down and confess. That just en-couraged at least one of them to lie to me. Knowing one of them was lying infuriated me. Not knowing who to punish the infractions began to accumu-late. I felt like I was trapped in a cycle of ineffective disciplining and my joy of parenting was being depleted.

It finally occurred to me that whether I got a confession or not, if an infraction occurred someone had to pay the price. This meant I had to do a little detective work and punish the most likely suspect, even if I was wrong once in a while. Allowing these infractions to occur without any conse-quences was more devastating than occasionally punishing an innocent child. It was not only unfair to the victim but also to the perpetrator. So I printed out a list of "House Rules," lined up all the children, and explained to them that any time a rule was broken someone would pay a conse-quence.

"Here are the house rules in their entirety." I announced, "If anyone of these rules is broken, someone shall pay a consequence, no exceptions. I will do my best to determine the most likely violator but even if I am wrong someone will pay."

There are ten rules. They are found in the scriptures in Ephesians; God's Ten Commandments. Here are the rules as God wrote them:

The Ten Commandments
1. You shall have no other gods before me.
2. You shall not make for yourself an idol in the form of anything in heaven above or on the earth beneath or in the waters below. You shall not bow down to them or worship them; for I the Lord your God, am a jealous God, punishing children for the sin of the fathers to the third and fourth generation of those who hate me, but showing love to a thousand genera-tions of those who love me and keep my commandments.
3. You shall not misuse the name of the Lord your God, for the Lord will not hold anyone guiltless who misuses his name.
4. Remember the Sabbath day by keeping it Holy. Six days you shall labor and do all your work, but the seventh day is a Sabbath to the Lord your God. On it you shall not do any work, neither you, nor your son or daughter, nor your manservant or maidservant, nor your animals, nor the alien within your gates. For in six days the Lord made the heavens and the

earth, and the sea, and all that is in them but he rested on the seventh day. Therefore the Lord blessed the Sabbath day and made it holy.

5. Honor your father and your mother, so that you may live long in the land the Lord your God is giving you.

6. You shall not murder.

7. You shall not commit adultery.

8. You shall not steal.

9. You shall not give false testimony against your neighbor.

10. You shall not covet your neighbor's house. You shall not covet your neighbor's wife, or his manservant, or maidservant, his ox or donkey, or anything that belongs to your neighbor.

At first the kids were excited as if I'd set them free. They asked me questions like; "These are the only rules right?"

"Yes."

"So we can do whatever we want as long as we don't break these ten rules?"

"Yes."

I saw grins and wheels spinning but it didn't take them long to realize that God had a pretty good plan when he laid down his Ten Commandments.

"Does staying out all night honor your father and your mother if they set a curfew for you?" I would ask. "Isn't saying you'll be one place with a set of friends but intending to ditch them and go somewhere else later lying? Certainly that isn't honoring your father and your mother. Is taking your brother's game without asking permission stealing?"

You can easily apply these Ten Commandments to most the rules you have established over your house and to the guidelines you use that help your children follow them. It is a simple plan to teach the kids how God's commands are designed to benefit us. This is how we should live in relationship to God and to each other. It is the breaking of these rules that cause trouble in our homes, our lives, and our relationships. Establish God's supreme law over your household and be willing to enforce them.

GETTING STARTED:

Take the time to meditate on each commandment and determine which infractions are being made in your home. Teach your children with love and consequences to come under the authority of these commands.

Instruct them how individual and societal consequences are incurred because mankind continues to break these laws God has given to us for our own benefit.

Although you should contemplate the areas of each command where you fall short, your perfection is not required to begin enforcing these commands in your home. Every infraction should come with a consequence. Grace can be given on occasion as well. When you do offer grace point out the natural consequences that have occurred; who got hurt, who took the pain for their infraction. Teach your child the consequences that cannot be undone by their actions and how that eventually comes back around and effects them.

Having a consistent discipline plan is imperative. A simple system of progressive discipline is a good place to start:

1. Remind the child of the appropriate way to behave.
2. Remove the child from the situation to a quiet, reflective place.
3. Restrict the child to a room or impose limits on privileges.
4. Re-earn privileges, which is necessary for chronic behavior problems.

The goal is always repentance, taking responsibility for one's action, and a change of future behavior.

If you don't have a confession, it is hard to get repentance. However, sometimes repentance is years down the road and some kids will allow others to be punished for them. Again remind your child how the consequences of their actions affect others and eventually themselves. The ultimate goal is for them to begin to see for themselves how their actions affect others, their relationships to us, and our relationships with others.

As children grow and mature, our methods of discipline grow to fit their ability to understand the situation. The transition follows something like this: Control/Discipline → Motivation/Rewards→ Consequences/Self-discipline→ Negotiations/Compromises → Advice/Letting go. As your children grow in understanding you will move from mostly control and discipline to more and more motivation and rewards. As they grow you will be able to teach them more about natural consequences and those consequences you impose. If the method you are using is not accomplishing the desired results, back up a stage or think about your expectations. Either your child isn't ready to assume the responsibility for that stage or you are not ready to give up your authority over the results.

The eventual goal is that your adult children will seek your advice but you will have to let go of the need to control them. However, you cannot abandon your authority while they still live in your home. Employ negotiations and compromises with adult children living in your home and letting go of some issues that do not compromise your values. You don't have to let adult children drink alcohol in your home if you don't agree with that but you can only advise them of what to do in their own home. In love, tell them how you feel and then let it go, let them make their own decisions.

With three or more children, more than likely you will be in several stages at once. I have a 16-year-old and an 8-year-old. While my 16-year-old was babysitting the 8-year-old, he was making his little brother squeeze through my chain-locked bedroom door and open it up for him. Eventually I had to tell my 8-year-old that a person in charge can not ask you to sin and I was going to hold him responsible if he went through the door again even if his brother asked him to. The next time it happened I told my 8 year old, in front of the 16 year old, to go to my room and wait for his swat. He was extremely upset and the 16-year-old asked me not to give him a swat because he was the one that told him to do it. I said, "Well, since the infraction was incurred and the punishment was a swat are you willing to take the swat for your little brother, because I cannot let the infraction go unpunished." He agreed, received the swat, and they have stayed out of my room ever since.

I am not advocating spanking or condemning it. This is a highly personal decision that parents need to make. If you choose it, please have a specific model in mind to avoid physically contacting your child out of anger. Insert a cooling off period into the plan that will in all cases separate the time of the infraction to the time of the punishment and allow you enough time to determine the best way to teach the child to correct future behavior. It's a good idea to try out other methods of discipline and ensure they are ineffective before implementing a plan for corporal punishment.

Some of you with teenagers realize that the opportunity to use discipline methods that were once effective with younger children, are no longer working. However, our responsibilities as parents don't end when our children become teenagers. It's a tough time because we are trying to change the method of parenting that took years to figure out at a critical time in our children's lives. And what used to work on teenager number one may not work with teenager number two. And frankly, that whole letting go thing is very difficult for parents who are not ready for a child who wants to play tug of war for independence years before we are ready to hand it over.

The hardest part of raising a teen is laying down the law and then getting out of the way and letting them make mistakes as they work through some tough stuff on their own. Starting with clear expectations, finding a good mix of motivation and rewards, without letting them bend our values as they reach adulthood will help you negotiate and compromise as you build a solid foundation for their launch into independence. No matter how rocky it gets if you leave the door open they will come back for advice but they don't always heed it. Let go.

Some borrowed phrases from natural horsemanship training will help you trot along the path a little more smoothly before they venture out the door.

"Make the right thing easy and the wrong thing difficult."

"Ask and allow."

"Reward and correct."

I know these phrases sound very simple and I intentionally used very simple words so you can use them as a mantra as you are in the thick of it. Horse trainers don't have time before the horse kicks to go back and get the manual. So be prepared. If you have a rebellious child, I can tell you the stress is too much for long-winded fixes. You will be repeating these mantras over and over again. Like horses, kids are not meaning to be bad most want to please us but they want to do it on their own terms. They are scared of growing up and yet, excited about being independent. So your job is to make the right thing easy and the wrong thing difficult. Be very clear what the right thing is and stand your ground. Ask and allow. Allow them to try to please you. Reward and correct. Compliment their effort no matter how small and then ask them again. Keep asking until they get it right.

If you do have a rebellious teenager, you will need to get a good support system going. Find someone who has raised a rebellious or strong-willed child that can listen to you, who doesn't mind you calling in the middle of the night when your daughter doesn't come home, and who will pray for you both. Find someone who will still be able to love your son or daughter after they put you through years of torture. Again stand your ground on what you know is right and wrong and remember, when they have convinced you it's all your fault remember it is not your fault. Stand firm on the truth God has shown you. Do your best to keep them safe from themselves and others. One day they will come back home and thank you.

Even though you aren't perfect you can still ask your children to aspire to improve. When my kids complain, "but you don't," they often hear another one liner I use, "It's a process." Remind them the goal is to be more and more like our leader and perfect role model, Jesus Christ.

Part of the process is to take a look at yourself, too. We all have room to grow more like our master so start with the house rules. Repent and determine in your own heart to come into compliance with each of God's commands. Repent of old infractions, request forgiveness directly from the person you wounded if possible. Be willing to forgive others that have wounded you in the past whether they have asked for forgiveness or not. Prayerfully seek guidance how to change and request strength from the Holy Spirit in your weakness. Evaluate all house rules you have and determine if they support the practice of the Ten Commandments. If not, consider whether they are just religious rules and impositions on your children or on yourself. Can they be eliminated? Allow love, faith, and hope to flow freely in your home.

AFFIRMATIONS:

☐ I have established the rules of acceptable behavior in my home.

☐ I have a consistent plan to enforce the rules of our house.

30 DAY PROJECT REVIEW QUESTIONS:

1. What is your current system of teaching and disciplining?
2. What about your current system of enforcing House Rules is working?
3. What about your current system of enforcing House Rules needs improvement?
4. List your goals in this area in your Home Management Notebook.
5. Choose one or two priority goals in this area to get started on or complete this week. Write them in your Home Management Notebook.

TOOLKIT:

➢ A Ten Commandments Chart, Form 11-1
➢ The Progressive Discipline Flow Chart, Form 11-2

SUGGESTIONS FOR FURTHER STUDY:

- ➤ *Parenting Your Adult Child* by Ross Campbell, MD, and Gary Chapman
- ➤ *The Five Love Languages* by Gary Chapman and Ross Campbell
- ➤ *Dare to Discipline* by Dr. James Dobson
- ➤ *The Strong-willed Child* by Dr. James Dobson

Day Twelve
PERSONAL SPACE

"I will drive out nations before you and enlarge your territory."

Exodus 34:24

Whose refrigerator is it anyway? It takes a lot of time to plan that weekly menu of meals, make the grocery list, shop, stock the fridge, and inevitably as you go to prepare the planned meal an ingredient is missing. Like the entire quart of cottage cheese that no one ate, yet sure enough when I went to make my Lasagna I pulled out an empty container.

My husband was always very territorial about the refrigerator. As the main cook, it was his domain. I didn't really understand that until it became my sole responsibility to keep it stocked with enough ingredients to prepare a meal each evening. I would have been more supportive in defending the ownership of the refrigerator domain had I understood his position as cook like I do now. Conserving resources is only one reason people claim domains and in this chapter we will look at the needs individuals have for their own spaces or boundaries.

In every home there are several types of boundaries that a home manager will need to evaluate. These boundaries include territory, personal space, privacy, and time. Territory can be defined as the physical domain in which a person feels they control or manage. Personal space is the physical distance a person requires for their comfort zone. Privacy relates to the sharing of information about an individual or their associates. Time is the balance between how much a person is allowed to have private reflection or adequate companionship. As you begin to look at the boundaries already established in your home, it won't take long to appreciate the need to plan for their design and defense strategies.

Territorial boundaries are a part of all life. Humans mark their territories as much as any animal and even plants claim territory and defend it. Many wars have started over territory disputes and it is inevitable that disputes in your home will arise over territorial needs. God recognized the need for humans to claim and rule over personal domains. In Exodus 34:24 he promised, "I will enlarge your territory." Jabez, in 1 Chronicles 4:10, cried out, "bless me and enlarge my territory."

Personal territories include bedrooms or areas of bedrooms, a personal shelf or cubby, backyard play equipment, or an indoor toy box. In Western society, every member of the family is usually assigned their own personal territories or an individual may lay claim to one. It is natural for territories to be defended by their claimers so the more you can define each territory, it's owner, or its rules for common use the better you will be in heading off conflicts over boundary issues. Some areas may be defined as "off limits" to certain household members and these definitions should be made clear through a strategic teaching method and by using consequences in love. In addition, once territories are commonly assigned to individuals a strategic plan to combat and deal with infractions is helpful. Some parents, often in Asian cultures, choose to expect less ownership and more sharing of individual territories. In any case it is important to become aware and consistent of how we are assigning and protecting territory so we aren't unintentionally favoring one child or family member over the other. In addition to human members of a household, it is important to assign territory or space to pets as well and train them to respect the boundaries they have been given.

Personal space is the average physical distance around a person that the Wiki-encyclopedia defines as 60 cm to each side, 70 cm in front, and 40 cm behind that a person in Western culture claims as a zone of comfort. It's probably easier to remember as the personal bubble of comfort that surrounds us. It is important for parents to understand that some children are not as comfortable with intrusions into their bubble as others. This doesn't mean the parent should never enter the bubble of a child who is standoffish but rather gently help them to increase their comfort with occasional hugs and other signs of affection. Everyone needs a hug now and then even when it is uncomfortable and yet, it is important to help a child increase their comfort zone in a gentle way so they learn to receive affection. But it is also important to respect this personal comfort zone during conflict.

When correcting a child, respecting their personal bubble can help you to be more effective and not cause the child to shut down. This is important for interaction between adult members as well.

Some children, as well as adults, will defend their personal space by lashing out at the invader. This is a natural defense mechanism. It is important to teach children how to avoid conflict during an invasion of their personal space. If they recognize their discomfort is a space issue they can learn to step back and increase their bubble.

Privacy has to do with the sharing of personal information about an individual or their associates. This issue becomes more pronounced as children enter their teenage years. It is a myth perpetuated among teenagers that they have a "Right to Privacy." Until a child is responsible for their self legally and financially, they can not claim a right of such privacy. However, it is important that a parent balance the need for a teenager to develop a sense of their own private life while maintaining a level of knowledge that will keep their child safe during a high pressure time of life for their child. Parents need to remember that they are responsible for all individuals in their home and especially for their minor children.

Two ways we handled the privacy issue effectively in our home was that the children knew they could maintain a level of privacy provided they obeyed the family rules. At anytime if they began to break curfews or engage in other rebellious behavior, their safety and protection outweighed their need for privacy. The second way was contrary to a common 'just close their door' parenting philosophy. At some point I realized that it was okay to keep cleaning my teenagers' room and they would not grow up to be messy adults if I did. When they are paying the bills for their own home, they will more than likely take ownership of it. As teens they often don't feel the need to keep my house clean and cleaning my teenagers' room was a great way to know what things were going on his life. You find out a lot cleaning a kid's room and they actually appreciate the tidiness and ability to worry about other things. I have found for most teenagers when they start yelling about you cleaning their room they are hiding something. This doesn't mean searching their dresser drawers or reading their diary; Trust me, you don't want to know everything.

I find regular visits to your kids' room are important and if you have a regular activity where the kids expect it, it is not so invasive. Weekly cleaning or vacuuming or laundry gathering, whatever regular activity it takes to give you an opportunity to check out their territory is worth it. While you're in there you can look for signs of how things are going in your child's psyche and communicate with them about any concerns you might have.

The fourth area of space is time. Everyone needs to be able to have some time alone for personal reflection and for some family members, time to learn how to be alone. Alone doesn't need to mean lonely but the only way to discover how to manage alone time is to have some alone time. It is important to see that kids are balancing their time between alone time and time for companionship, and between doing activities alone or with friends and time with family.

Personal space is a matter of balancing the following:
♦ Personal and family time
♦ Quiet space and activity space
♦ Personal prayer and family prayer
♦ Personal retreat/refuge and coming to someone for comfort

Questions to ask:
1. How do you envision each family member's territory?
2. Is there a specific territory assigned for each person or are all areas shared?
3. How do you deal with arguments over territory?
4. How are "Off Limit" spaces defined and violations defended?
5. Are there places adults don't go? If so, how do you monitor what happens in that territory?
6. How are rules for privacy weighed against safety for minors and other household members?

AFFIRMATIONS:
• Our home has a good balance between shared and private spaces.
• Our family has a safe balance of openness and privacy.
• Off limit areas are well-defined, justified, and respected.

30 DAY PROJECT REVIEW QUESTIONS:
1. What is your current system for personal space in your home?
2. What about your current system for personal space is working?

3. What about your current system for personal space needs improvement?
4. List the goals your have for this area in your home management notebook.
5. Choose one or two priority goals you can complete or get started in this area this week. Write these goals in your home management notebook.

TOOL KIT:

- Personal Space Chart

SUGGESTIONS FOR FURTHER STUDY:

- *The Hidden Dimension* by Edward Twitchell Hall

Day Thirteen
FAMILY READINESS

"It will be good for those servants whose master finds them ready, even if he comes in the second or third watch of the night."

Luke 12:38

"My teacher said to bring my own pencils tomorrow," your angel blurts out while you tuck her into bed.

"Honey," your husband asks, "don't we have any more stamps? I just need one."

"I am out of paper," your son nags.

"We're out of staples and my teacher said my papers had to be stapled."

At what point do you retreat and pull out your hair? Did you forget where you put those pencils you bought at the start of the school year when they were on sale? Instead of hopping into bed as you planned, you hop in the car to find a store open at this hour to restock those pencils and supplies at convenient store prices.

Why do you need to stop what you are doing to reload the stapler or get your husband a stamp or even restock your son's paper supply? If you set up a system, they could do this all by themselves. It's called a Family Resource Room. Family resource rooms take on a variety of sizes and styles depending on your home and your needs.

GETTING STARTED:

Choose a location to dedicate to the storage of white paper, notebook paper, spiral notebooks, filing folders, and other papers that you want to have on hand to refill school supplies and your home office. In addition to paper, you can keep an office caddy at the same location stocked with typical office supplies your family will need to refill their desks or use on occasion. Basic items include paper supplies, stamps, staplers and staples, scissors, and other office and school type supplies.

If you like having printed reference material available for times when the computers are tied up, keep it near the rest of your family's resources. Reference materials may include a family dictionary, a family bible, a thesaurus, a road atlas, and possibly other maps and references if you have the room. I like to dedicate an entire shelf in the library for our reference material and it includes phonebooks and member directories from school and church as well as printed maps of our favorite hiking trails.

Another shelf is set aside for the paper and supplies storage. A large closet shelf or storage cabinet also works well. I like to keep the references and supplies close together and near the home office. However, I keep the family resource area clearly separated from my home office. I don't want the kids to be in the habit of rummaging through my desk to find their supplies. So I keep the two spaces very distinct even if they are in the same room. My desk is off-limits!

If you don't have room for a home office, you can dedicate a corner of the dining room or kitchen to store these supplies and build a small corner shelf for your reference shelf. I have even used an entire shelf in a hall linen closet as well as devoted part of my kitchen pantry to office supply storage. The important thing is to dedicate a space and use it consistently for that purpose so you can find those pencils you bought on sale when you need them.

 I like to buy the notebook paper and spiral notebooks for school and home use when it is on sale in the fall because it is so much cheaper. However, I often couldn't find it when January came around and the kids needed a refill. Then I would have to pay over 75% more for it and eventually found I was storing large amounts of yellowing paper. Do you know where the milk is right now? Just like you know where to put the milk when you get home from grocery shopping, you will know where to put your extra supplies of notebook paper and pencils. Do you know how to tell if you are out of milk or not? A designated Family Resource Room works the same way as the empty milk shelf in the refrigerator. You know by looking when it's time to refill.

Other locations for the Family Resource Room may include the home library, a craft room, or hall closet. The home library is probably the most ideal place for the Family Resource Room. It is ideally suited for reference materials and is easily adapted to bulk paper and supply storage. A second choice might be the craft room with a portion of a cabinet dedicated to supply storage. A closet in the home office works as well if you don't mind the kids coming in and out of your office space. If you want to eliminate extra traffic, use the closest hall closet to your home office. This puts the bulk storage conveniently close to you yet keeps intruders out of your office.

Location is also dependent on how freely you want the supplies to be accessed by other members of the family. I have a closet solely dedicated to office and school supply storage. I keep a small amount of supplies near my desk and the rest in the closet. School supplies and a small resource caddy are located on the bottom shelf that the kids are allowed to access at anytime. I check the shelf before we make our monthly trip into the discount store so I can restock if necessary. I keep other supplies that they must ask permission to use, like glue and scissors, on the upper shelves. I have labeled their shelf attractively, "Kids Supplies," so they realize the boundaries.

The reference material shelf is now located on the first bookcase as you enter the home office. It keeps the traffic away from my desk. Having it near the door of the office, gives the kids easy access to the references and is still handy for me to use working at my desk. I enjoy them peeking in for a quick chat while I am working on a book project.

Whether the family resource room is a shelf, a closet, or a stack of plastic drawers, it is a micro-zone. You designed your home's functional zones in Chapter 2 to assign functions to each space in your home. Now you are beginning to narrow down all the nooks and crannies in each room. Eventually you will define a purpose for every drawer and space in your home. Some references maybe more appropriately stored in the zone in which they are used. Such as cookbooks, which are often stored on a dedicated shelf in the kitchen. Computer manuals may be stored on a dedicated shelf, filing cabinet, or drawer in your computer desk. Use your Home Management Notebook to list these dedicated micro-zones in your index.

Setting up a Springboard:

In addition to the resource rooms, which include the bulk office supplies and reference materials, setting up a "Springboard" helps ensure the things you've prepared and packed for the day make it out the door. The Springboard is a ready room or mounting platform zoned to hold items waiting to go out the door. This is where the backpacks and briefcases wait after being loaded up with their supplies. We have coat hooks about shoulder high to an eight-year old that hold backpacks, lunch packs, and jackets. I also have a slotted cubby shelf. I've assigned a cubby for outgoing mail and one to hold misdirected mail for each adult child they can check when they visit. Another short bookcase is by the door to hold items that are left by friends or packages to be shipped. We use the Springboard as we prepare for trips and all items not to be forgotten are placed there. As soon as we think about an item that needs to go out the door with us, whether to school, work, a friend's, or on a trip, it is put on the Springboard.

"Can I get my crockpot back?" my friend asked during a phone conversation.

"Sure, I'll put it on the Springboard," I assured her. While we finished our conversation, I picked up the crockpot that had been stored in my kitchen so long I thought it was mine and placed it on the Springboard. Next time I went to visit it would be there to remind me to take it along. As it turned out, she visited me before I got a chance but there it was on the Springboard and on her way out the door I said, "Oh, don't forget your crockpot."

As long as it makes it to the Springboard, no item is forgotten.

AFFIRMATIONS:
- ❖ Family resources and supplies are stored in a designated place.
- ❖ Supplies are stored in a way that is easy to inventory and restock.
- ❖ A Springboard has been designated and utilized at or near the front door.

30 DAY PROJECT REVIEW QUESTIONS:
1. What does your current family readiness system look like?
2. What is working with your current system?
3. What improvements are needed for your current system?
4. List the goals you have this area in your Home Management Notebook.
5. Choose one or two top priority goals from your list to accomplish or get started on this week. Write them down in your Home Management Notebook.

TOOL KIT:
- ➢ Family Resource Room Inventory Checklist

SUGGESTIONS FOR FURTHER STUDY:

- ➢ *The Official Scrabble Players Dictionary* by Merriam-Webster
- ➢ *Webster's New World Thesaurus* by Charlton Laird
- ➢ *NIV Family Bible Duo Tone - Clubs* by Zondervan
  (with room for Family Records)
- ➢ *Mini Timelines of World History* by Jane Chisholm

Day Fourteen
DELEGATING RESPONSIBILITY

"If a man will not work, he shall not eat."

2 Thessalonians 3:10

"If I would have been a horse-woman when my children were little, I would have broken big jobs down into smaller tasks more. I would have asked, gotten out of their way, and allowed them to try more. If I would have been a horse-woman when my kids were little, I would have made doing the right thing easier for them and doing the wrong thing much more difficult. If I would have been a horse-woman when my children were little, I would have rewarded them with praise on every real try and made sure I didn't reward them when they didn't try. I would have found an opportunity to always end our encounters on a good try just like I do for the horses I now train.

If I would have been a horse-woman when I was married, I would have complained about my husband's messes a lot less and just hired a ranch hand to clean up after him. I would have soothed his aching muscles more, asked for more of the things he was good at giving, and found more reasons to praise his good tries. If I would have been a horse-woman when I was married, I would have understood the need for some studs to be dominant and think they are in charge. I would have gotten out of the way and let my husband be the leader. I would have learned to lead from within the herd and been more thankful to have a good leader.[1]"

Using natural horsemanship to train horses is all about motivating your horse to want to give in to your leadership. Jesus talked a lot about servant leadership and concentrating on helping others more than telling other people what to do. What does that really look like if you are trying to teach your children to take responsibility for their selves or soliciting help from your spouse? What I learned from training horses is this:

1) Ask and then get out of the way. Evaluate the try. If it was even a little better than before, accept it and reward it.

2) Keep the pressure on until you get a try. Ask, get out of the way, and look for a try. If they are not trying, increase the pressure while making the wrong thing (not trying) more difficult than trying. If there is a try, make it easier to complete than quit – usually with teenagers that means getting out of the way, for younger kids it might mean pitching in and helping them. "Oh Jonathon you are doing great can I help you finish up?" Tell a teenager what they did right about the job and back off without pointing out their shortcomings. This can yield surprising results next time they help out.

A lot of parents make the mistake of being inconsistent in their expectations which leads to a battle of wills every time you ask a kid to do their fair share. If they have not had to do it for three months, they don't recognize it as their fair share. Then after a battle ensues the parent decides it is not worth it, it's easier to do it their self. Another three months go by and then the parent realizes they are running ragged doing everything themselves and want help. Another battle ensues when mom or dad decides to change the rules. Determining what responsibilities each family member should have and teaching them how to develop regular routines to complete their chores minimizes the battle of wills and increases the cheerfulness of your helpers.

GETTING STARTED:

It's never too late to start. Begin by determining the habits you wish to change both for you and for your helpers. Begin with small steps, developing a habit such as put your clothes in the laundry basket instead of on the bathroom floor. Present the new idea, give a motivator, ask, allow, reward the try or up the pressure.

"Jonathon, I put a laundry hamper in the bathroom for you to put your dirty clothes in. I would like you to use that instead of the floor. That way I can make sure I get all your clothes when I do laundry and you'll have your favorite clothes, fresh and clean to wear when you want them instead of trying to find them on the bathroom floor. So if I find your clothes on the floor I am going to come and get you, ask you to stop what you are doing, and go pick them up."

In order to help teach these new habits, you have to develop a new habit of reviewing the tasks regularly. Right after shower times, check the bathroom floor. If they have not put the clothes in the hamper you can click off the TV, delay the snack, or somehow get the child's attention. If you find they did it without asking, make sure you praise them for their effort. Check regularly and respond appropriately. Always end on a praise report after they have done the task. And don't get in the habit of rewarding them before and asking later, for example, "You forgot to pick up your clothes, as soon as you're done with your ice cream get in there and pick them up, okay?" Instead, check before snack time and say, "As soon as you've picked up your clothes off the floor, I'll make the ice cream."

If you had to ask, allow them to respond without nagging. If they still don't pick up the clothes it's time to up the pressure. Make them go to bed without snack while you pick up the clothes for them. Tomorrow night repeat the process until they respond with less and less pressure such as only a reminder.

It is okay to help your child out with their chores from time to time. When you do their chores, maintain your expectation they do them by letting them know you did them for them. "I noticed you were distracted so I took your plate to the kitchen for you. I'd really appreciate it if you would remember to do that next time." Expect a thank you, and remember to thank them for their work as well.

Foundational habits include dividing hours of chores up in to very small steps that can be split up among family members. To begin building foundational habits teach household members to continually clean up after themselves. If that is all you get done you are miles ahead on a typical chore list that includes picking up trash, laundry, dishes, and other clutter that family members leave behind. So this is where I like to start even if it means I do all the scrubbing, dusting, and vacuuming.

A step-up from foundational habits, are assignments of household responsibilities in which individuals contribute to the upkeep of the household over and beyond what they do for themselves. This might be scrubbing a toilet or raking up leaves in the yard. You've made your daily routines list in Chapter 5, now it's time to get a little help with it. You can also solicit help with the repair list you'll be making in Chapter 15 from your spouse and from the kids as they get older and more skilled. Begin thinking about ways other members of the household can help you get some of this done using their skills, talents, and interests.

Like our horse-woman wrote, she would have asked her husband to do more of the things he was good at giving. This is great advice for any of your helpers. Why not ask them to do the things they either have a vested interest in or things they are good at doing or enjoy doing? For a long time I couldn't understand why the kids didn't care if the house looked great for our company but I felt so obligated to ensure they learned to care about the house like I did. Then one day my teenage daughter yelled at me during the height of an ensuing battle over household chores, "You act like I care what this house looks like, it's your house mom not mine." Well that kind of burst my balloon because all these years since the kids were little, I thought of this as our home. After that comment, I realized no one really taught me to care about my home I just did because I picked it out, I pay the mortgage, I show it off to my friends, it's mine. It changed the way I motivated the kids to help me keep up with it. Someday they will have their own home and be self-motivated enough to care for it. Right now, I have to figure out other ways to motivate them.

I started looking for the things they enjoyed to do and asked them to use their gifts and talents to help around the house. My daughter likes to organize things so she often helped me with spring cleaning where we moved furniture, cleaned under it, and rearranged it. My 16-year old son often got in trouble starting fires when he was younger so when we moved to the country he became the official trash burner. In any way I could I learned to delegate things I knew the kids would enjoy doing, do well, and help me eliminate another task on my load. Instead of taking all the leftover chores, I reserved a few I enjoyed for myself, like mowing the lawn on the riding lawn mower. If you like a little solitude to the hum of an engine, this is one chore you'll fight for.

Praise is an excellent way of rewarding the efforts family members are making. Get in the habit of noticing what they are contributing, especially the things they do that you didn't ask for. Let them know you notice and appreciate their efforts. Other methods for rewards include reward charts. We started a chart to reward my 8-year for brushing his teeth twice a day. The reward is putting a star on the chart in the morning and the evening. He enjoys watching the stars add up and visually being able to see the progress he is making. We can both easily see the times he missed. I started something similar on the family school calendar to let my 16-year old visually see how many days he was actually tardy for school. Just seeing it was enough to change his behavior because he enjoyed seeing a week full of stars meaning he had gotten to class on time every day.

If you want to do monetary rewards, having a task check off list is an excellent idea to help the kids make their chores add up to a nice commission. Give a dollar amount to each task on the list and when they have completed their assigned tasks in a cheerful and timely manner, they get paid that amount. They can earn extra money by doing other tasks on the list. The key to this method is pay for the tasks as they are completed and let them be responsible for their own entertainment funds. No longer allow yourself to be the ATM machine for them. Answer the question, "Can I have $5 to go to the movie?" with, "You can go to the movie if you have $5. I am not your ATM machine. You need to earn your money first then you can spend it."

The Family Chore check off chart can be broken down in monetary values. You can also use it to record payment. I put a check on the chart as they complete their work and each check is worth a given amount which varies depending on how much money is in the budget that week for personal spending. I take the allotted money and divide it by the number of checkmarks and hand out the money accordingly. Then I make each checkmark into an X to indicate they have been paid for that amount. Pay for bigger jobs is negotiable. For example, I pay my older son a set amount to put up a new run of fence or my youngest son can earn a little extra by washing the vehicles. If you don't have the cash other incentives, like picking the family movie or a trip to a park to play can be used. The key is to agree on the incentive beforehand and deliver it promptly after the job is done and not before.

Motivation is also important when dealing with gaining help from your spouse. Read the book of Esther, she planned an entire evening meal and allowed time to prime her husband before asking for his help. This is a great idea. At least it beats, shouting out demands or nagging. Be realistic when dividing up responsibilities with your spouse. What is he already accomplishing? What does she do well or enjoy doing? What do you both enjoy doing together? What do you do well or enjoy doing? What is left over and how can you motivate your spouse to help you accomplish it? Remember as the household manager you must motivate not dictate.

According to Marcus Buckingham in *First break all the rules,* "to get the best performance out of people you need to reveal their strengths, not focus on their weaknesses." The art of successful delegation comes out of knowing and utilizing people's strengths. Individual personalities don't change a whole lot, so find out what they are good at and enjoy and then take advantage of it to ease your burden. If no one is able or willing to do it, consider hiring it out.

AFFIRMATIONS:
- ☐ I know the strengths, talents, and interests of household members and can apply that to help accomplish household tasks.
- ☐ I notice the things others are contributing to the household and let them know I appreciate their help.
- ☐ I motivate others to do their fair share with clear expectations and rewarding their efforts. I allow them to try and increase the pressure or consequences when they don't.

30 DAY PROJECT REVIEW QUESTIONS:
1. What is your current system of delegating responsibilities?
2. What about your current delegation system is working?
3. What about your current delegation system needs improvement?
4. List the goals you have for this area in your Home Management Notebook.
5. Choose one or two priority goals to accomplish or get started on this week. Write them down in your Home Management Notebook.

TOOL KIT:
- ➤ Family Chore Check Off Chart

SUGGESTIONS FOR FURTHER STUDY:
- *http://riders4c.blogspot.com/2006/01/thank-god-im-horse-woman.html*
- http://www.ksbrixey.com/?p=326
- *First break all the rules* by Marcus Buckingham

Day Fifteen
HOME REPAIRS

"Finish your outdoor work and get your fields ready, after that build your house."

Proverbs 24: 27

Have you ever tried to sell your house? You add that extra touch as you clean it up for your realtor to take a peek. You think you have a gem that could list for top dollar but after the initial walk-through with your listing agent you wonder how you ever allowed your family to live in such a wreck. There are more holes in the walls than you ever noticed. The door that won't close right is more than a nuisance now that you have to pay to have a new door jam installed. The combination of paints you so masterfully decorated the living room with last fall are an eyesore and those walls need to be primed and painted with a neutral color before the house can even be shown. Every room of the house is deluged with destruction; there is no way you can get it ready to show in time and on your budget.

Luckily, we are not always under such pressure but we can feel overwhelmed when it seems like every room of the house dawns disaster. Standing in a foot of backed up sewer water I called my dad for his advice and secretly hoped for a little sympathy and encouragement. "Welcome to the world of home ownership," he chuckled.

"What should I do?" I asked.

"Well," he pondered, "the way I see it is you either fix it or call someone who can. I sure wouldn't leave sewer water standing in my garage for long."

I guess that meant he wasn't planning on coming over and fixing this for me so being the new homeowner it was going to be up to me to find a solution. Fix it or call someone who can because this definitely couldn't wait. It didn't take long for the 'fix it or call someone who can' list to grow and soon I was juggling time and money trying to keep up with it all. Needless to say, the door that didn't close right wasn't on the top of the list and kept getting put off. At some point I realized, I was going to have to live with a few things but some things I put off, like red flashing lights in the garage, meant financial or physical disaster. We didn't know we had a sewer pump and that the red flashing light in the garage was hooked to it. It periodically went off telling us, had we known, the holding tank in the front yard was not draining. It usually stopped flashing so we ignored it. Eventually the intermittent problem became permanent and I ended up standing ankle deep in sewer water, red light flashing, holding the phone to my ear as my father chuckled, "Welcome to home ownership." This one probably couldn't wait any longer to get fixed.

If you own a home, you are going to have a few home repairs to make. If you let them go, this list can grow exponentially. The most overwhelming part of home ownership is a daunting never-ending home repair list. Accept the fact that tackling home repairs is a process similar to doing laundry. There are always going to be things on the list that need to be done. It doesn't mean let them pile up until you are living in a home worth well below the price you are paying for it. The key is prioritizing and completing as many as you can on an ongoing basis. Using a prioritized home repair schedule can help you keep up.

GETTING STARTED:

The home repair schedule is a comprehensive list you make of all the repairs that need to be done in your home. The list is categorized by room and prioritized by using a cost plus future cost method. In other words, how much will it cost to repair this item plus how much would it cost to put off the repair of this item. Not replacing a ten-cent washer can mean thousands of dollars of water damage down the road. If you have a water leaking of any kind, that usually moves to the top of the list, second only, to something like a gas leak or some other life-threatening defect. Of course immediate threats to life or property should be dealt with on the spot. After you've dealt with immediate threats, schedule repairs in order of their priority using the cost plus future cost method.

Our home repair list is made using a property tour we call "Ranch Rounds." It is tagged after the old cattle days when cowboys rode the property boundaries and checked to make sure all the fences were in good repair. We tour our property at periodic intervals and take notes of all the necessary repairs, problem areas, and goals we have for each part of it.

Begin the process with a legal pad divided into three columns: Rooms/Area; Repairs and problem areas; and goals. I use one page for the interior and another for the exterior. Move from one room to the next jotting down problem areas you see. Don't forget the bathrooms, closets, and cabinets. When you finish inside, move outside. Look at the exterior of the house, the patios, driveways, and gardens. Keep your initial list to cross off repairs as you make them and to compare to your next list. After you have compiled a list of notes from each room, ensuring no immediate threats, choose the highest priority on a cost-plus-future-costs basis in each room and list it on your home repair priority schedule.

I try to keep making repairs in every room on a regular basis by listing my top priority in each room. If not, I find that one or two rooms tend to get neglected and always put on the bottom of the priority list. This is a great list to bring along to the hardware store with you especially if you jot down the measurements and sizes of items you'll need to do the repairs. If you see what you need you can pick it up and repair it on the spot.

Ranch rounds need to be done regularly not just when you've completed the repairs on your current list. Conduct a ranch round at least every six weeks. Compare the previous list to the new one you make up so you don't overlook anything you spotted before. Priorities change. The gutter repairs that may not seem like a big deal during the summer drought become more pressing as the rainy season approaches. In addition, anytime you are feeling overwhelmed with things breaking down, do a quick ranch round and re-prioritize your list. Use the list to cross off the repairs you've made so you can see how much progress you are making. If someone ever says, "Let me know how I can help you," just hand them your home repair priority schedule and they can help you complete a few tasks off your list.

AFFIRMATIONS:

- ☐ I have set up a regular schedule to conduct ranch rounds and build a home repair list.
- ☐ I have listed my top priority repairs needed in each room or home area, inside and out.
- ☐ I have set up a regular schedule to make needed home repairs.

30 DAY PROJECT REVIEW QUESTIONS:
1. What is your current system for scheduling and completing home repairs?
2. What about your current home repair system is working?
3. What about your current home repair system needs improvement?
4. List your goals for this area in your home management notebook.
5. Choose one or two priority goals to accomplish or get started on this week. Write them in your home management notebook.

TOOLKIT:
➢ Home repair and problem area list.
➢ Home repair priority schedule.

SUGGESTIONS FOR FURTHER STUDY:
• *The Complete Photo Guide to Home Repair: With 350 Projects and 2300 Photos (Black & Decker)* by Creative Publishing International

Day Sixteen
FAMILY COMMUNICATIONS

"Our people must learn to devote themselves to doing what is good, in order that they may provide for daily necessities and not live unproductive lives."
Titus 3: 14

"Still here…" my son's highly irritated voice beckoned from the receiver, "Is anyone going to pick me up?"

"Oh I thought your dad was picking you up," I apologized.

"No, you said you would and I've been trying to call for over an hour." He explained.

"I'm sorry I couldn't find the phone. Now, tell me again where you are?"

Cell phones are great for walking around and getting things done while you are chatting. They are not so great when you want to answer the phone and you left it on the charger in the other room. You rush in from another room to answer the phone and you missed the call. There has to be at least one phone in the house that is permanently attached or you will drive yourself mad dashing for to the phone to answer it whenever it rings. If you don't have a landline, use a Bluetooth phone for your base phone.

In a house with four kids, it was exhausting trying to keep up with everyone's schedules. I had a hard time remembering who had to be where when and who had a ride and who didn't. My husband only went to pick up kids when he was told to so that meant I was in charge of coordinating it all. During the start of baseball season it was complete madness. I had two boys playing baseball, one girl playing softball, and my kindergartner playing t-ball. Having cell phones would have helped with the older kids but would not ease the distance between ball fields when they all needed to be there at the same time.

"Go look on the school calendar," I say with confidence. "I am sure he needs to be at practice by 6pm."

"Where is the school calendar?"

"It's in the front hall hanging up by the phone."

The phone is our llingo for the only phone you can count on to be there. "The phone" means the one attached to the wall with the cord that is set up in the Family Communications Center. The purpose of the family communications center is basically scheduling and coordinating. It is the hub of incoming and outgoing messages, of everyone's schedules. It is where our individual day planners come together, so that everyone can get to where they are going, be where they are suppose to be on time, and no one will be left waiting for hours to be picked up. It is designed so that no one will miss important family occasions like Grandpa's 100th birthday party or Aunt Carol's 25th Wedding anniversary. The Family Communications Center is a micro-zone used for coordination between family members to keep track of their schedules and their incoming and outgoing messages.

When my kids got older and got part time jobs, they would try to convince me that I forgot to tell them about an important family event such as a 100th birthday party or a 50th wedding anniversary. And honestly with their schedules they easily missed announcements of the sort. However, I explained to them they were responsible for knowing what was on the family calendar and planning their activities around it including asking for the day off from work for important family events. They needed to discuss conflicts with me before the night of the event and together we could determine how to resolve them. So my job was to make sure all events got put on the family calendar and their job was to review it on a daily basis.

In addition to the family calendar and a phone, the family communications center includes a message board, a cork board for tacking up announcements, and a small filing system for team schedules, calling trees, and family phone numbers.

Things you need in the Family Communication Center:

- ☐ A permanent phone with a cord attached, a speaker phone, or Bluetooth home phone system.
- ☐ An answering machine or call notes/voicemail.
- ☐ A Calendar to schedule appointments for family members (does not include task scheduling). Sync family members together using a smart phone app or online calendar such

as Google Calendar.
- ☐ Phone Books and/or a Family Phone Number List
- ☐ Message Board (white board or chalk board)
- ☐ Post it notes, Pen, Pencils, Markers
- ☐ Bulletin Board and push pins (to pin up team schedules, invitations, reminders.)

The family communication center needs to be set up in a location where household members frequent readily and it is highly visible. Preferably near the phone that gets answered most frequently but definitely by one you can count on being there. Consider the design of your home for the best location. Often the Kitchen works best but an entry way near the front door may work as well. Our communication center is combined with the springboard we discussed in chapter 13.

Begin setting up your center with the things you already have on hand. Use your system for awhile and see how it works. Then after sufficient testing and a revising period start adding some interior design features to what is working. Without testing the system you don't know if what you are proposing is even going to work. And you waste a lot of money. In other words don't decide to design your system at the store looking at someone else's ideas. Decide what you need and design it before you go to the store. Once you know what works you can take your time and find something not only efficient but also aesthetically pleasing and of higher quality. You can spend more knowing it is going to be a lasting system not just another mass produced idea that doesn't work for your family.

AFFIRMATIONS:

- ☐ I have a family calendar I check daily and a regular schedule to keep it updated with school, work, and family events and appointments.

- ☐ Household members know where the family calendar is. They know they are responsible for ensuring their events are on the calendar and for coordinating their own schedules to attend important family events.

- ☐ The family communication center is in place and all family members frequent the location to check and leave messages, coordinate schedules, and check the family calendar.

30 DAY PROJECT REVIEW QUESTIONS:

1. What does your current system of family coordination consist of?

2. What about your current system of coordination is working?

3. What about your current system of coordination needs improvement?

4. List the goals you have for this area in your home management notebook.

5. Choose one or two priority goals you can accomplish or get started on this week. Write them down in your home management notebook.

TOOLKIT:

 ➢ The Family Calendar

 ➢ The Family Communications Center

SUGGESTIONS FOR FURTHER STUDY:

- Organize Your Family's Schedule In No Time by Valentina Sgro
- The 7 Habits of Highly Effective Families by Stephen R. Covey

Day Seventeen
STEWARDSHIP
Simplifying Systems and Managing Material Wealth

"For where your treasure is, there your heart will be also."
Matthew 19:21 (NIV)

A neighbor of mine stopped by unexpectedly, a gentleman from down the street. I courageously invited him in and sheepishly cleared a spot on the couch for him to sit down. It was my first day off and I was just preparing to start my daily chores. Laughing off the mess in the living room as a hectic week, I sat down on the other couch. As he started to talk, I noticed an article of clothing just six inches from his shoe. Not hearing a word he was saying I was trying, without looking at the item, to determine what it was. Dreadfully, I realized it was under clothing, mine! I blinked, smiled, said, "Uh huh."

Luckily the whole room was full of clothes and clutter because it had been a hectic week I consoled myself. I moved my attention to a pile of towels near the television, grabbed the pile, and accidentally dropped the top towel on top of the underclothing. I excused myself, lifted the pile again and heaved the pile down the stairs, smiling at my guest. "Don't forget the towels." I hollered down to the unsuspecting children in the basement recreation room. They had no idea I had asked them to do the laundry but par for the course ignored me anyway. This time I was thankful.

I just hadn't noticed the under garments on the living room floor because at the time there were too many other piles of clutter blocking them out. There were U-haul boxes of papers, junk, small appliances, lots of books, and supplies. We were moving in and had been for a while. For the last six months I had joked with my visitors about U-haul being our decorating theme that ran throughout the entire house. How long would that be funny? I was already tired of it. I wanted my new house new again. Not cluttered with the junk I brought here from my past life.

There is nothing as exciting as a new house when you first get the keys. You run from room to room, there is room to breathe. There is room for all kinds of possibilities. Freedom! Then the U-haul boxes start showing up, the old furniture that you didn't realize was so soiled, and the broken down toys show up that distract from the freshness of a new home. Moving would have been a great time to get rid of all this junk . We just didn't have time to sort through it to find the treasures among the heaps of stuff we'd accumulated in our old overly cluttered home.

Whether you are in a new home or in your old home, creating room to breathe will make your home fresh and alive again. If you aren't moving anytime soon, then you have time to start the process. I am going to start the process of de-cluttering a little different than you might expect. I am going to start with the assumption that you have already de-cluttered. Now, how do you keep it that way? What causes the clutter to accumulate and what processes do you need in place to keep it from happening?

My sister-in-law is the most anti-clutter person I know. She keeps nothing and gets very agitated when my brother wants to keep something that does not have an immediate use. It is great for us because her son is one year older than my son so she has this system of weeding out the clothes he's outgrown, putting them in shopping bags, and surprising me with these wonderful gifts every six months or so. My son and I are both delighted. An efficient system of letting material goods come in and go out will keep your home breathing, feeling fresh and like new.

The pit falls to the material flow system occur when we hang on to items because we might need them in the future. Just before I became pregnant with my youngest son, I had finally gathered up my eight- year- old son's baby clothes. I had taken them to my nephew's mom and proudly said, "I won't be needing these anymore." What I didn't know is I was already pregnant with my little surprise package. I swore I would never get rid of anything again. But what I didn't realize is that God had already put in place ten-fold the replacements in clothing than I had given away. I have never to this day needed for one stitch of clothing for my surprise package. The key to letting things go in and out of the house is to realize and trust that your future needs will be met. You don't have to hang on to the old stuff because it will only gather rust and get older. Let it go, let someone else use it.

GETTING STARTED:

Learning to let go is hard but it is easier when you know someone else will value what you are letting go of:

1. Admit when something is trashed and you are not ever going to get around to fixing it. Throw it away.

2. Sell items online at ebay.com, amazon.com, or your local free trade and flea markets. Designate a place to store items that are listed for sale. If they don't sell in a given amount of time, (I will list mine twice) then give them to charity.

3. Freely give when you see a need and you have something stored for future use. This is the future use you stored it for because someone else can put it to use now. List your items on trade notices that you belong to. Form and join free trade organizations such as your county's facebook Swap and Talk.

4. Set up a giveaway system whenever you can. For example, if you know a young man that is two sizes smaller than your son you now have a direct line give away for any clothes as he outgrows them.

5. Give to charity. Keep an inventory of your gifts, their fair market value, and get a drop off receipt for tax purposes.

6. Boxes: If you have the storage space, keep original boxes of items that you know will outlive their useful value to you and still have value to someone else. These are also useful if need the box to return for repairs. Recognize items that you will use up and do not keep their boxes. If you choose to keep boxes for shipping items you sell on the internet, break them down and store them flat. Keep your boxes in a designated storage area such as on a shelving unit in the attic just for reusable box storage.

7. Determine what is important. Anything you keep should be something you think is worthy of your time to maintain. If you love it and it brings you joy, display it or rotate it through displays. Keep it repaired or up to date. In her book, *Use What You Have Decorating*, Lauri Ward says, "Think Collections." Keep things if they add value to your collection. Limit your collections to a few that you really want to maintain and display. Display collections in groups of five pieces, store the rest, and rotate them periodically to give a fresh look to your rooms. Designate a place to keep your collections safe and with reasonably easy access. This is similar to what you do for your Christmas decorations stored in one place in the attic. You can set up attic shelves for your collections

as well and rotate them throughout the year. Caution: Do not store candles or other heat or cold sensitive items in the attic.

8. Utilize other systems for storage such as the public library for books and the internet for information. Use Lauri Ward's collection idea for your home library. Only maintain a library of books that add value to a collection of books you enjoy owning or are frequently using as references. Most other books are as accessible as your library card.

9. Designate a temporary place for memorabilia and make it easily accessible for short scrapbook sessions. During these sessions update a page or two in a scrapbook with the goal of having all memorabilia, newspaper clippings, and photos saved in well-themed and displayed books.

Think about how items flow through your home. Do they come in, stop, and accumulate after their usefulness or value has passed or do they flow through helping keep the pulse of the home alive? Is what you choose to store easily identifiable and accessible? If you store wood and screws, do you go to the hardware store or to your storage area when you need wood and screws for a project?

Set up a rotation system for charity in your home.

1. A place for items that you intend to give away. A large, clean trash can with a trash bag in it works well. Tape a piece of paper on the side to write down items as you place them in the bag.

2. Schedule a drop off/delivery day each month or mark the charity's pick up date on your calendar.

3. For clothes, have your give away bags in the laundry room where you fold your clothes. As you fold up clothes, any item that is too small or that no longer fits in your identified wardrobe goes into the charity bag.

4. Identify other areas of weakness. You will know them by the piles they create in your house. Set up systems to allow these items to flow through your house. Is it magazines piling up? You may choose to have a small magazine rack that holds your current issues of subscription magazines or mail order catalogs only. As the new issues come in, the old one goes out. Decide what to do with old ones.

5. Throw them out and refer to it again from the periodicals sections of your local library or at www.findarticles.com

6. Clip any articles you want to keep. Put them into a subject notebook where you will store your collection of articles around that topic or put the article in a scrapbook.

7. If you will frequently refer to past issues, you may choose to collect all issues of a certain magazine (Have an extremely good reason for this!!). Get a large 3 ring binder and either hole-punch the magazine or purchase magazine holders for 3 ring binders. Immediately place your new issues in the binder. We keep two subscriptions in binders; the Perfect Horse and Zoobooks. The Perfect Horse comes already hole punched. Zoobooks we remove the poster, then hole-punch it and put it in my son's binder where he enjoys adding new issues to his collection each month.

Do you have stacks of books? Sell them on Amazon.com. I put a stack of about 10 books up a couple weeks ago. I really wasn't too hopeful they would sell because there were tons of similar used books up there and some for as little as a $1. But I just put them up and so far two of them have sold. I made about $19. It's not a get rich quick scheme but it beats dusting them and I got more for them than in a garage sale.

How many spatulas do you own, what about can openers, or shoes? Each month designate one area of your home and simplify it. For example, in the kitchen set out all your pans and decide how many skillets you need. Certainly not more than four if you only have a four burner stove. How many roasting pans? Line up your small appliances and honestly evaluate the ones you will use. Store small appliances by frequency of use—the least used in the back and the most frequently used near the front. Of course, if you use them at least once a week see if you can find an attractive spot for them on the counter.

Do you have a closet full of clothes and nothing to wear? It might be time to overhaul and simplify your wardrobe. Here are a few simple steps to complete the wardrobe plan:

1. Sort your clothes in accordance with the items in the wardrobe plan outlined below.
2. Choose the best fitting of each item in the recommended quantities. Give away the rest.
3. Make a shopping list of the items you need to purchase to complete the wardrobe plan. As your budget allows, shop for one or two of the items on your list. Instead of entertaining yourself at the mall and overspending, shop with a purpose.
4. If you lose weight, take the opportunity to give away a pair of jeans and purchase a new pair. As clothes wear out, replace

them with a more comfortable pair or higher quality replacement.

THE WARDROBE PLAN:

The Mississippi State University Extension recommended the following basic wardrobe plan in neutral colors for women:

- ☐ One three-piece suit (jacket and skirt or pants)
- ☐ One blazer or jacket
- ☐ Two basic skirts
- ☐ One pair of classic slacks

- ☐ Two blouses or shirts

- ☐ One tunic-type top
- ☐ One or two dresses
- ☐ One sweater or cardigan
- ☐ One pair of casual slacks or dress jeans
- ☐ One hostess dress or gown
- ☐ One year-round coat with removable lining

This basic wardrobe is simple, flexible, and can be mixed and matched together to create a week's worth of outfits. From this you can add special sets of clothing to fit your lifestyle such as swimwear, camping clothes, special occupation outfits, or hobby clothes.

When it comes to material wealth, less is more. Keep only items that you cherish or use and have the time and passion to care for properly. Store the items that you only use seasonally in an organized storage system. Get back to basics when it comes to clothes, kitchen utensils, and tools. Keep your favorite items and give away or sell your duplicates. Utilize public storage systems such as the library for periodicals and books, online resources to replace mail-order catalogs, and the hardware store to keep the necessary items for your next project.

AFFIRMATIONS:

- ➤ I have organized the possessions I choose to keep and care for into collections that hold value and meaning for my life.
- ➤ I have created a plan where material goods flow in and out of my home on a regular basis according to their useful life.

30 DAY PROJECT QUESTIONS:

1. What does your current system of stewardship look like?

2. What is working with the way you currently let material goods flow through your home?
3. What improvements need to be made to your Stewardship system?
4. List the goals you have for this area in your Home Management Notebook (HMN).
5. Choose one or two top priority goals from your list to accomplish or get started on this week. Write them down in your Home Management Notebook.

TOOLKIT:
 ➢ A Basic Wardrobe Plan
 ➢ A Material Goods Flow Plan
 ➢ A Collection Inventory and Storage Plan

SUGGESTED READING FOR FURTHER STUDY:
 ➢ *Use What You Have Decorating : Transform Your Home in One Hour With Ten Simple Design Principles -- Using the Space You Have, the Things You Like, the Budget You Choose* by Lauri Ward
 ➢ *Looking Good: A Comprehensive Guide to Wardrobe Planning, Color & Personal Style Development* by Nancy Nix-Rice and Pati Palmer
 ➢ *Details Men's Style Manual: The Ultimate Guide for Making Your Clothes Work for You* by Daniel Peres, the editors of Details magazine

Day Eighteen
HEALTH RECORDS AND PLANNING

"Dear friend, I pray that you may enjoy good health and that all may go well with you, even as your soul is getting along well."

3 John 1:2

I never worried much about the cats. Once in a while they might drag home a bird or a lizard tail but other than that they kept pretty much to themselves. They were all fixed and in the spring a reminder came in the mail and I would take them in for their annual vaccinations. I never kept track of it because I thought I would let the veterinarian office handle that. After all, I got my annual reminders for each cat when they were due for a visit.

One summer afternoon the door bell rang and when I opened the door, the whole cat plan unraveled.

"Your cat just bit our friend's daughter and they have taken her to the hospital," my neighbor informed me. "We need to know if the cat has had her rabies shots. If not, the cat is going to have to be quarantined."

As I madly rummaged through every pile of paperwork in my house not long after that conversation, I answered another ring at the front door. Two patrolmen were inquiring about the state of the cat. "Yes, the cat had rabies shots I am just not sure of the last date. I am looking for her tags."

The patrolman was very kind and understanding and offered a solution to my paperwork nightmare, "Why don't you just call your vet. They should have a record of that."

"Great Idea," I thought.

However, the clerk at the veterinarian's office said she couldn't find any records of them ever seeing my cat.

"What? Did you try Grand Teton? You send me a reminder card for her visits every year. How can you say you have no record of her?"

As the animal control officer drug my frightened cat out from under the patio, more of the story began to unfold. We were surprised to hear her little kittens crying since she had been spayed by the same animal clinic. Know we knew why she might have acted in an unusual way that day. And Her out of character behavior made sense as the whole story was recalled one witness at a time.

My daughter had taken the cat into the neighbor's yard to show her off to the girls playing there. The neighbor's daughter threw the cat on their dog and as the other girl tried to rescue the cat , our cat bit her. Our cat then ran back and hid under the patio with her kittens. The story turned tragic as we tried to reach the kittens that were safely tucked away underneath the slab of concrete and out of reach. There was no compromise with the law and Grand Teton was not allowed to be quarantined under the patio with her kittens. Instead she was removed and taken to a veterinarian's office for 10 days of observation while her kittens starved to death without her under our patio.

Guilt-trip on mom who could have prevented the whole kitten tragedy by presenting the officers with a little piece of paper that showed the cat was current on her rabies shots. Still curious, how a veterinarian's office that managed to send out annual reminder cards to one "Grand Teton" could not find a record of such a cat in their files. A cat they had supposedly spayed and kept current on annual shots for over five years.

Other health records are important too. How many times have you been asked to produce your child's immunization record for a sports' physical or for summer camp? How many times have you had to call and get another copy of those records? Guilty again! When my husband was disabled we had to reproduce records that went back over 5 years to prove he was eligible for social security disability payments. He had seen over 7 doctors on his long trail of finally being properly diagnosed. Because we were able to at least come up with copies of bills from three different states, we had the name and numbers of those doctors who had seen him. Luckily they kept better records than the veterinarian office and were able to inform the judge advocate about his past clinic and hospital visits.

In addition to health records, you will benefit from having a health plan or what I like to call a health schedule. I use the task tracker form that you will find in chapter 4. If you have pets, you know they must have annual vaccines, dewormer, and tick and flea treatments. Most doctors recommend annual physical exams for the aging (yes that is all of you over 35 but who's counting) and for women there is an annual Pap smear and for those over 40 the recurring mammogram. Men have their checks, too, like prostate and cholesterol checks. Infants and preschoolers have a series of immunizations and preventative checkups to schedule. Of course, there are the dental routines as well. Recommendations change so check with your doctor and your vet to help you determine which items pertain to your household and set up your tracker schedule for each family member and pet.

GETTING STARTED:

Start a health file in your home office filing system for each member of your household and each pet as well. Gather all your medical records. You do not need to keep every bill (payment of services is kept in financial files, this file, *The Health Record*, is to document actual health records not financial records), unless for tax purposes, but do keep documentation that will track every doctor's visit, the results, symptoms, diagnosis, and treatment. Start a health card for each family member and pet. Health cards schedule preventative checkups and keep track of doctors' visits, tests and results, illnesses, and treatments. The card is a quick reference and tracking system that your documentation files will back up with the "proof." If you haven't been keeping good health records then start with the most recent treatments and checkups and work backwards filling in what you can determine from past documentation and recall. Put a star by anything you recall without documented proof to indicate it is to the best of your recollection but not a documented fact. Keep a health card in the front of each individual folder of documentation. Take your health card schedules and transfer reminders onto your Household Scheduler for health check ups, dental routines, and veterinary returns, include immunizations and preventative check ups.

AFFIRMATIONS:

- ☐ I have a health record for each family member and family pet.
- ☐ I have a system for keeping the health record updated.
- ☐ I have contact information for each servicing professional, for future reference.

30 DAY PROJECT REVIEW QUESTIONS:

1. What does your current Health plan and records system look like?

2. What is working with your current health plan and records system?
3. What improvements need to be made to your current health plan and records keeping system?
4. List the goals you have for this area in your Home Management Notebook (HMN).
5. Choose one or two priority goals from your list to accomplish or get started on this week. Write them down in your Home Management Notebook.

TOOLKIT:
  ➢ The Health Records
  ➢ ealth Planning Schedule

SUGGESTIONS FOR FURTHER STUDY:
*note: if links change, try to go back to the root address such as www.cdc.gov or type the name in your search engine.
  • National Library of Medicine, www.nlm.nih.gov/
  • National Center for Infectious Disease, www.cdc.gov/healthypets/
  • American Veterinarian Medical Association,   www.avma.org/communications/brochures/animal_health.asp

Day Nineteen
DECISION MAKING

"Again, I tell you that if two of you on earth agree about anything you ask for, it will be done for you by my Father in heaven. For where two or three come together in my name, there am I with them."

Matthew 18:19-20

I love meetings. I enjoy the details of making up agendas, brainstorming, determining priorities, setting goals, and assigning action items. I love whiteboards and dry erase markers, chalkboards, and newsprint with scented markers. I love coordinating day planners and just the whole idea of sitting around a table and kicking around ideas, thoughts, and knowledge with like-minded colleagues.

I was sold on Franklin Covey's Seven Habits of Highly Successful Families and gathered my family around the living room to develop our Family Vision Statement. What a disaster! It was obvious that my family was not into thinking about ideas as I was. We couldn't even sit around a board game together without being at each other's throats. So the first thing the kid's asked to put on the agenda was "get rid of family fun nights." URGH! They had no intention of brainstorming a family mission statement but they would stay if they could discuss raising their allowances. That was not on the agenda!

Eventually, I learned that it was better to have consensus meetings. In other words, I come in with the plan and let them tell me what they think of it. Even better yet, I just go to each one of them individually and get their opinion if they have one. Often, even my husband, didn't have an idea or input at our meetings. Decision making therefore became my job. If a decision needed to be made my husband told the kids, "Go ask your mom." If I made a decision without him, my husband always said no to the idea. Then later he would think about it and let me know he thought the idea was fine. The kids picked up on that as well and quit asking him and just came to me.

You are probably not surprised how many decisions must be made in one day. What is for dinner? Where do you want to go this weekend? Whose turn is it to wash the dishes? Whose turn is it to play a game? What happens to a kid who misbehaves? Can we have a friend over? Can I spend my allowance? Do you want to move? Oops! I forgot to ask the 7-year-old. We're moving anyway and he is not happy because I didn't ask him for his opinion.

GETTING STARTED:

Evaluate how you plan future events. Do you include every member of the family? Also, if there is a conflict, how is resolved? Planning should include every affected member at some level: maybe just input during a brainstorming period, maybe certain decisions at their level of delegated authority and interest, or maybe putting them in charge of a complete phase of the planning. Also remember to poll family members for feedback after the event as well. Seeking ideas from those affected or able to influence can solve conflicts and problems in the household.

Steps To Conflict Resolution

1. Choose a mutually acceptable time and neutral place to discuss the items in conflict. Be clear about what will be discussed and what will not (Do not allow bringing up a laundry list of past conflicts).
2. Let the other person be heard first. Remember to listen twice as much as you talk. Explore completely the other person's perspective on the situation without defending or analyzing. Restate what you heard to make sure you understand correctly.
3. Use "I" statements to express how the actions or behaviors of the other party make you feel. Do not blame but rather share your feelings and perspective.
4. Ask the other person how they would like to see the situation change. Restate what they said to make sure you heard them

correctly.

5. Express how you would like to see things change by adding on to what the other person is hoping for without changing it whenever possible.
6. If there is a conflict between what both parties want, state them clearly and ask for ideas from the other party on how they could be resolved. Try to develop a plan that will resolve the conflict and accommodate the needs of both parties. Often these means compromise on the part of each party.
7. Restate and get agreement on the new plan as well as decide on a follow up time to discuss how the new plan is going. All agenda items do not have to be conflicts or problem solving. Use family meetings proactively to increase family effectiveness in stewardship, servanthood, and discipleship. Sometimes, especially with young children, it's best to meet with family members one-on-one and then combine all the discussions into one solution or action plan.

Not all family time needs to be to resolve problems or plan. Healthy conversation and feeding into each other's lives is important. Put away the smartphones and other electronics and tune in to each other. It is recommended that couples spend at least 15 minutes devoted to discussions with each other daily. As soon as you or your spouse come home from work, sit down on the couch or in a regular conversation area; no kids, no TV, no newspapers, and take some time to tell each other how your day is going and encourage each other. Let the kids know that this is sacred time for you and your spouse. If you are single, spend this time with the Lord. Do not neglect this couple time because you don't have kids in the house.

Plan some conversation time with each household member every day. The family meal is an excellent way to do this regularly. Set daily routines where you can spend one on one time, even if it is just a few minutes with each family member. Many parents do this at night when they tuck the kids in for bed. If bedtime is stressful, choose another time when things are less chaotic.

Other family time ideas: Weekend outings, Family night board games, or ongoing puzzle tables that lure family members into the project. Create relaxing, conversational areas like a back patio deck and see how many family members are drawn to it when you retreat there for peace and quiet! Sometimes these spontaneous family meetings are the most enriching moments in family life. Put regular date- nights with your spouse and/or kids (even grown up kids) on your household scheduler.

Allowing family members to contribute to family planning is not meant to relinquish your authority over your household. Without you remaining in charge, chaos among the ranks will develop. There is a lot of peace that children and family members have when those in charge take charge. This can be done in a loving and engaging way but yet standing firm when things really matter. Remember to praise in public, criticize in private.

AFFIRMATIONS:

- I include all affected family members in the decision making process at some level without relinquishing proper authority over my household.
- Without nagging, I use conflict resolution steps to solve family problems.
- Our family members have a lot of opportunities to spend quality time together to share their hopes and dreams with each other as well as get feedback on struggles they might be going through.

30 DAY PROJECT REVIEW QUESTIONS:

1. What is your current decision making system?
2. What about your current decision making system is working?
3. What about your decision-making system needs improvement?
4. Write down your goals for this area in your Home Management Notebook (HMN).
5. Choose one or two priority goals that you can accomplish or get started on this week. Write them in your Home Management Notebook.

TOOLKIT:

➢ Conversational/gathering areas
➢ Family times
➢ Conflict resolution steps

SUGGESTIONS FOR FUTHER STUDY:

- *Respectful Parents, Respectful Kids: 7 Keys to Turn Family Conflict into Cooperation* by Sura Hart (Author), Victoria Kindle Hodson
- *Facilitator's Guide to Participatory Decision-Making* by Sam Kaner, Lenny Lind, Catherine Toldi, Sarah Fisk, and Duane Berger

Day Twenty
INDIVIDUAL DEVELOPMENT PLANS

"But one thing I do: Forgetting what is behind and straining toward what is ahead, I press on toward the goal to win the prize for which God has called me heavenward in Christ Jesus."

Philippians 3:13-14

One day, a little voice, said to me, "If money was not an object what would you want to be when you grow up?" Now, the fact that I was in my early thirties did not hinder me in any way. All my life I had just went with the flow and no one told me I was steering. When all my friends were graduating high school and going to college to pursue their lifelong dreams, I went into the Air Force because I had no clue what I wanted to do and honestly, had never even thought about. I know, we did career exploration in high school and my dad constantly told me, "You need to have a skill you can sell." But for some reason I never took the leap from there that made me decide what kind of career I wanted to pursue in college.

So I took the ASVAB and scored high in electronics and consequently was put into an electronics job. That lead me to the career I maintained for nearly twenty-one years now. I can't say that I mind my job, actually I rather like it and I'll just say it suits me. But for many years I was not so happy with it and pursued other sources of occupations. I took inventories and personality tests and all kinds of surveys to determine what would make me happy professionally. I went back to school and got my Bachelor's degree in behavioral sciences and then went on and earned a Master's degree in counseling psychology. And then kept working in the field of electronics because I financially couldn't make the jump to my chosen career.

But what I realized through the process is that the answer to my dissatisfaction in life was not necessarily my job but it was the way my job fit into the rest of my life. I learned that dissatisfaction in one area had spilled over into my otherwise fulfilling career in electronics. You can not name one thing that makes a lifetime satisfying but rather the way our lives are balanced spiritually, physically, environmentally, and mentally will determine more of your life's overall satisfaction and purpose than anything.

Life Balance Wheel

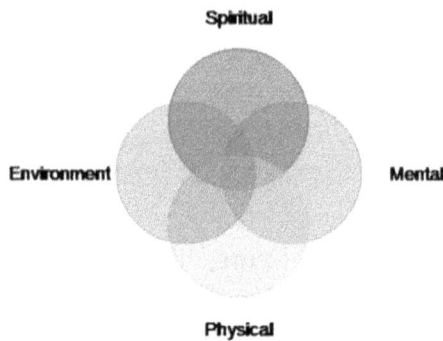

Spiritual

Environment

Mental

Physical

Figure 20:1 Life Balance Wheel

It is not how much education you have, your degrees mean nothing if they add nothing to the overall balance of your life. I do not regret my education because I enjoy gaining knowledge but what I have learned is that balancing and developing all four areas of my life has made my life more satisfactory and guess what, increased my satisfaction in the career that happened to me without my planning it. I am good at what I do and with a more balanced life I enjoy it much better by understanding how it fits into the rest of my life.

If you have children, it is your God-given responsibility to train them up. That may or may not include home-schooling, that may or may not mean sending them to college, and that may or may not mean paying for them to have music lessons, dance lessons, or expensive summer camps.

What it means is that you guide them in individual development areas such as spiritual training, character building, career preparation, and responsible self-management. It also includes helping them explore and discover their gifts which we will discuss more of in chapter 26.

The individual development plan is a great way to develop a plan for every member of your household to develop the knowledge, skills, and competencies that he or she needs or desires. It is a proactive way to help them grow towards their goals and to train them up in areas that are important to you. The IDP is a way to organize and set priorities for learning, development experiences, and character building. It will help each individual improve their performance in their currently assigned tasks, learn new tasks, assist in exploring and acquiring competencies for career development or work preparation, prepare them for increased household responsibilities, and actively pursue God's calling on their life.

The IDP helps the individual and the household manager establish objectives that support both the household's objectives and the individual's needs and goals. It is a clear guide for working toward long-term goals. Information in the IDP helps you find ways to help each other learn new skills and will allow you to evaluate the way household members can share their skills with each other.

The IDP is something that each individual should develop, review, and modify on an ongoing basis. This is the form where you set your goals for the upcoming year in all areas of your life from academics, career preparation, job improvement, character building, gifts and talent development, emotional development, physical health, and all areas in between. It is helpful to review the form at least once a month to determine if you are staying on track or need to modify the plan. Develop a new plan for each individual at least annually at the beginning of either the academic or the calendar year which ever works out best for your family. Keep the form as a record of training, education, and experience acquired for use on job interviews or setting new goals.

GETTING STARTED:

The form will ask you to set a short range goal and a long range goal. Start with the long range goal. It is a general statement about where you want to be in three to five years. Start on a separate sheet of paper writing a 5- year vision statement. Describe what your life looks like in five years, what's different from your current life, how do you spend your day and your time, how do you earn a living, etc? You can use the life balance wheel to help you think about areas of your life you want to include in this vision statement. When your done try to sum up what you wrote in a one or two sentence statement and write it on your IDP.

Individual Development Plan			
For:	Created on:		Updated:
Long Term Goal (3-5 years):			
Short Term Goal (1-2 years):			
Steps to Short Term Goal:	What it will take from me	Resources I will need to help me	Target Date to complete step

Form 20-1

Your short range goal(s) is a general statement of what you can accomplish this year to help you move toward that long range goal. Parents should work with children to determine mutual goals that they can support in addition to parental objectives for their children's growth.

Once you have written out what you wish to accomplish in the next year, break it down into developmental steps you will need to take to reach that one year goal. Use the chart to indicate the objectives, the activities, and the timeframes in which you will accomplish them. List any resources you will need to accomplish the goal and then begin to think about ways you can tap into those resources.

All family members should have an IDP that the family leadership and partnership can support each other in. You are never too old or too young for an IDP. The younger the child the more parental involvement is needed in the development of the IDP. Adult children may also appreciate parental coaching in an IDP. Sharing the plan with adult children can help them know you are still supportive of them and you can offer your wisdom and experience to help them overcome obstacles and support their achievement of their long term goals. I say this with the understanding that the wisdom and experience you are offering is to point them to the resources they need not to be their resource handout.

Don't forget to update your own IDP. It's a lifelong process that through prayer and diligence will afford you much satisfaction in achieving a well balanced life.

Sample questions to ask your self:
1. What is my goal?
2. What do I need to learn?
3. How will it help?
4. How can I learn it?
5. What method works best for me?
6. What resources and supports are available?
7. How will I know I learned it?

AFFIRMATIONS:
- Each family member has created an Individual Development Plan I can support.
- Individual Development Plans are reviewed monthly and revised annually.

30 DAY PROJECT REVIEW QUESTIONS:
1. What is your current system for planning individual development?
2. What about your current individual development planning system is working?
3. What needs improvement in your current system of planning individual development?
4. List goals you have for this area in your Home Management Notebook (HMN).
5. Choose one or two priority goals from this list you would like to accomplish or get started on this week. Write them down in your HMN.

TOOLKIT:
- ➢ Individual Development Plan, Form 20-1
- ➢ Life Balance Wheel, Figure 20-1

SUGGESTIONS FOR FUTHER STUDY:
- ➢ *What Color Is Your Parachute? (most recent) A Practical Manual for Job-hunters and Career-Changers* by Richard Nelson Bolles
- ➢ *The Sacred Romance Drawing Closer To The Heart Of God* by Brent Curtis and John Eldredge

Day Twenty-One
HOME VISION

"If they had been thinking of the country they had left, they would have had opportunity to return. Instead, they were longing for a better country—a heavenly one."

Hebrews 11: 15-16

A friend of mine was diagnosed with diabetes and as a result she radically changed her lifestyle and developed some healthy habits that are making a big impact. Now, I have known her for almost thirty years and she seemed to have healthy habits years ago, too. She was always the one that convinced us to take a walk around the block after dinner and walked so fast none of us could keep up. She was the one drinking the diet pop and watching her diet. However, she didn't seem to be losing weight and at times seemed to be gaining more than losing.

However, after she was diagnosed with diabetes things changed. She started working out and watching her diet very closely. And it is obvious that what she is doing in front of us is what she is doing when we were not looking because she has lost the weight and is looking and feeling great. So I had to ask myself, what is so different this time? What about all those exhausting dashes around the block and diet pops, why weren't they working?

The answer came in her response to the many compliments she receives about how great she looks. She replies, "I don't want to die." It's not our methods that work or don't work but the motivation behind the method that makes or breaks it. Although exercise and diet combined are the main ingredients to lose weight and feel great, there are many methods to achieve that. But any method will fail without proper motivation. If you feel like your failing at any lifestyle change, think carefully about the motivation you have for changing. Keep the motivating factor prominent in your mind and with the right mindset you will succeed.

Vision and mission statements serve to keep our motivation key in our minds and available in our planning. My friend's vision statement, "I don't want to die," mirrors the vision of her in five or ten years, "ALIVE." That is her vision and her mission is to take control of her diabetes by counting carbs and exercising to make sure she stays healthy and alive. The Vision statement captures a quick look at the future or rather your destination and is easily recalled in times of great temptation. The mission statement is what you are actively doing to get to your goal.

Having a vision and mission statement for your home is an excellent way to stay motivated to keep up with all the things we have been doing so far to put your house in order. If you do not know where you want to go, you probably won't ever get there. A vision statement is a brochure you create about your destination. You can look at the brochure and imagine what it will be like when you arrive. A mission statement includes all the details about what you will bring, when you need to catch a flight, which plane you will get on to ensure you make it there, and prepare you for the stops along the way. The mission statement is the flight plan you make to ensure you reach your destination. I'll board flight 1478 at 9:30pm on May 19th. I'll stop in Dallas and change to flight 558, and then arrive at my destination at 6:30am on May 20th.

Some organizations consider their mission statement their purpose but in our context and some would agree, we call the purpose the 'why' and the mission the 'how' and the vision is the 'where.' The vision statement quickly identifies where we are going, the mission statement explains the kind of things we should be doing to get there, and the purpose is why we are doing it. I like to keep the vision statement very short and easily remembered. The mission statement is designed using a formula I learned in Laurie Beth Jones' book, *The Path: Creating your Mission Statement for Work and for Life*. And the purpose statement can be anywhere from fifty words to a page in length.

The example below is the vision, mission, and purpose statements we have designed for our ranch:

> The Vision statement of R4C Ranch is "Preparing Riders for Christ." The statement encapsulates our mission and our purpose in something easy to remember and repeat back over and over to keep us focused and directed on our destination.

The Mission statement is also easy to remember if you know the formula that I'll share later. The Mission of R4C Ranch is to mentor, inspire, and equip families, corporations, and churches to live passionately for Christ, prepared for his return, through experiential training with horses and campfire retreats.

The purpose of R4C Ranch is to share God's love with all that are drawn here by the Holy Spirit and to serve them with all we have as the Lord leads us. Our hope is to allow others to draw near to God as the animals, the birds, the earth, and the fish teach and instruct them about whom the Lord is and what He has done.

As you can see the Vision statement captures a picture of what we hope we are doing. It was established before we even bought the property, a vision of our future. It is so easy to remember that anyone who works with us can easily repeat it and have a sense of what we want to accomplish in a nutshell. The Mission statement expounds on the vision by giving a clear idea of what we are doing to make the vision come true. The purpose is the ultimate motivating factor to even design the vision and mission statement in the first place.

Designing a purpose, mission, and vision for your home takes a little creativity but be patient and let it develop over time. Start by thinking about the three parts: purpose, vision, and mission. You may already have one or more of the parts designed in your head and just need to put it in words. If not, begin by thinking about the underlying purpose for your home, what you would like your home to be like in five years, and the things it would take to get there. Be sure you choose the things you are passionate about to use in your statements. If you don't like entertaining, don't make that one of your mission verbs.

GETTING STARTED

Jot down some ideas about the underlying purpose of your home. I'll list some ideas but certainly these are not all-inclusive and may not be congruent with yours. The purpose of my home is to be a refuge for the lost, a place of peace and refreshing for my family, a place to entertain friends and family, and where I will teach my children to follow God's calling on their lives. Keep jotting down ideas until you have a list of at least twenty ideas and then pick three to five as your priorities. If you can, limit the purpose to those five ideas.

Next think about your ideal home; imagine day to day life in your home in five years as soon as you accomplish the ideal home. What does it look like? What are you doing? Jot down these ideas. In five years my home will be buzzing with activities, grandkids, foster kids, and family and friends. I will be mentoring other believers and conducting small group bible studies. It will be clean, fresh, and orderly and prepared for Christ to knock on the door at any time. Although my kids will be grown and moved out, they will be visiting. Keep writing again until you have about twenty statements or more of your home on the list. Then think about the purpose statement as well as the vision lists for your home in five years. Do you see a pattern forming around these ideas? The idea is to create a statement that will capture these images in your mind in one statement that is easy to remember.

"My home will be used to make ready a people prepared for the return of Christ."

Having your purpose and your vision statement in mind you can develop a mission statement. Some find it easier to start with the mission statement and that is okay, too. You can do that as well. You can do these in any order and you can always come back and revise a statement until you get one that sticks.

Adapted from Laurie Beth Jones', *The Path: Creating your Mission Statement for Work and for Life*, which I recommend reading to create and understand your mission statement, we will develop the mission statement using three parts: the 'what', the 'who', and the 'means'. Look at the list of action verbs (appendix) or choose a few of your own. First circle the verbs you most enjoy doing. Then narrow down the list to your three favorites. Such as the three I chose for the Ranch's mission statement: mentor, inspire, and equip.

My favorite three verbs:
1.
2.
3.

Then decide one to three of your favorite nouns (data, people, or things) that you enjoy working with and would like to influence such as my family, businesses, horses, children, or women. Again you make your long list of favorite things and groups to work with and after coming up with at least twenty narrow the list to your favorite three.

The three I chose for the Ranch's mission were: families, corporations, and churches because I was want to influence individuals in their places of leadership. Possibly you won't influence people at all you may also choose to influence data or things or a combination of each of them.

My favorite three spheres of influence:

1.

2.

3.

Next you will need to add the means. This is how you want to do the verb you chose to the nouns you chose. In my case, how I want to influence them. In other words, this is the result you hope to achieve. I wanted the leaders I work with to live passionately for Christ. In addition I wanted them to be prepared for His return.

You can stop there as well and have a nice mission statement.

The mission of the ranch is to mentor, inspire, and equip families, corporations, and churches to live passionately for Christ.

If you have specific methods you intend to use for that mission then you can add the 'by statements'; how will you mentor, inspire, and equip them. The methods we use at the ranch are through experiential hands on training with horses.

An example of a home mission statement using this format could be:

The mission of our home is to <u>welcome, refresh, and equip</u> our <u>family, friends, and all</u> who enter our home <u>to face their daily battles</u> by immersing them in God's grace and truth.

Now we have designed the vision, the mission, and the underlying purpose for our home. Write them down in your home manager's notebook and review them at least monthly. Revise them as necessary. Memorize your vision statement so in the heat of the battle you can rattle it off your tongue and remember what success looks like. I suggest posting your home vision and mission statements in a prominent place to remind and share them with all that enter your home. Get the buy in of all household members by lovingly teaching them the vision and mission. If possible, include your spouse and other motivated adults in the creation process of these statements. It is a good idea to have a personal life vision and mission statement before you start the collaborative process of designing a vision and mission statement to ensure that the final product is congruent with your own personal life statements.

Life statements will keep you in touch with your inner desire and give you a framework for what success looks like. Your vision is the destination. Your mission is your purpose. A purpose statement is somewhat of a combination of the two. These are great for short-term goals that step by step help you achieve your overall mission and vision. A motto is a short phrase that is easy to memorize. After you have set down your long term (the next three to five years) and your short term (this year) goals, you can develop a motto to help guide your tasks or projects. One of our projects is to help people get started living passionately for Christ. For some people, their situations seem so hopeless they can't imagine what abundant life looks like. We developed the motto, "One step out of stuck," to help them acknowledge any progress they make and understand that abundant living is a process not a destination. Another motto, "Preparing Riders for Christ," is a quick way to remind us of our vision and mission. In this case, riders are leaders who first learn to be a leader of their own horse and then learn to lead an army for Christ.

Samples statements:
Vision: "Make ready a people prepared for Christ's return."
Mission: "The mission of our home is to welcome, refresh, and equip our family, friends, and all who enter our home to face their daily battles by immersing them in God's grace and truth."
Purpose: "The Purpose of our home is to be a lighthouse beacon for the lost; a place of peace and refreshing for our children, our friends, and all who enter here; and where we will teach our children and grandchildren to follow God's calling on their lives."

AFFIRMATIONS:
- ☐ I have a written purpose statement for my life and home.
- ☐ I have written a vision statement that captures what I hope for my life and home to be like in five years.
- ☐ I have written a mission statement to help me start creating that vision today.

30 DAY PROJECT REVIEW QUESTIONS:
1. What is your current Vision and/or Mission Statement?
2. What about your current Vision and/or Mission Statement is still helping you set priorities?

3. What would you like to change about your current Vision and/or Mission Statement and how it shapes your priorities?
4. List the goals you have for this area in your Home Management Notebook.
5. Choose one or two priority goals from this list you would like to accomplish or get started on this week. Write them down in your HMN.

TOOLKIT:
- ➤ Action Verb List, Form 21-1
- ➤ Data, Things, People List, Form 21-2

SUGGESTIONS FOR FURTHER STUDY:
- ➤ *Jesus CEO : Using Ancient Wisdom for Visionary Leadership* by Laurie Beth Jones
- ➤ *The Path: Creating Your Mission Statement for Work and for Life* by Jones
- ➤ *The 7 Habits of Highly Effective People* by Stephen R. Covey

Day Twenty-two
ACTIVITY SPACES

"Come with me by yourselves to a quiet place and get some rest."
Mark 6: 31

As children reach their teens and want their independence it seems like you can never engage them in any meaningful activity anymore. No longer do they want to curl up with you in bed and read a good story. It's rare they enjoy staying home on Friday night and playing board games but try to sneak off to the bathroom and sure enough they knock on the door with a question that just can't wait another second to be answered. It's as if they do not notice your presence as much as they do notice your absence.

Create the environment and they will come. Ever noticed how when you clean a room and move on to clean the next one, everyone goes to the clean room and messes it up. Everyone loves the atmosphere in a clean space and they are drawn to it. You can't schedule board games with teens but you can create an environment that is conducive to board games and they will be drawn into it. Try inviting a few friends over to play blurt and see how many of your teens want to join in.

Quality time is hard to plan. It happens by being in an environment that generates activity that leads to quality time. You can create these environments throughout your home. Create the environment and they will come and so will the quality moments.

I created one such environment with a backyard patio table I bought on clearance at an outlet store. It was large with a glass top and one chair for each family member. After work I would spend at least thirty minutes relaxing at the table with the intention of reading my daily scriptures and praying over my family members. It was so peaceful and quiet and fresh and full of God's presence. The kids gravitated to the table and soon I would be surrounded by all of them and engaged in spontaneous discussions about school and their situations that furthered my ability to pray for them. No one was forced to come and spend some quality time with mom but the peaceful atmosphere lured them there.

In chapter two, you set up functional zones that serve a purpose or function in your home. This chapter is an extension or tweaking of that concept in order to create a balance of activity, conversation, and quiet places in your home. You have probably already done this with multi-media. You probably have a TV viewing area and if you are like many Americans you've gone overboard with the TV viewing areas. Not every room of your home needs a television. Actually the opposite is true. You need areas that are quiet to contrast with the multi-media of televisions, stereos, video games, and computers. In addition there are other activities besides television the family could engage in. A project table with a puzzle or something family members can contribute to on a pop in, pop out basis is a great idea.

Create atmosphere in areas you used to just take for granted. Have dinner at the table with fancy tableware, a nice table cloth, fresh flowers, and candles. A soft light in the corner of the living room with a comfortable chair can create a reading nook. My friend and her husband put too recliners with a table between them in their bedroom as a space for them to get away and read. They were surprised how often they would end up meeting each other there. The enjoyable conversations they had there would have otherwise been missed in their hectic two-career daily lives.

Create a balance throughout your home of conversation and activity zones inside and out. Ambience or environmental zones are either quiet zones (sleeping, reading, resting), conversational zones (peaceful, minimal distractions, relaxing), or activity zones (multi-media, cooking, dining, storage, recreation, crafts). You don't have to have 2,000 square feet to create a balance of these zones. Some zones can be used for all three ambience levels but not at the same time. If you share a multi-media room with your conversation areas, you can use an entertainment center with doors and close them to "put away" the television and promote conversation.

Here are some questions to ask as you think about the zones you currently have and the one's you would like to create:

- Are the activities of the room distracting you and your guests from conversation?
- Do you have conversation areas set up and separated from activity zones outdoors?
- Do your conversation areas contain 4-8 seats that focus attention of each one inward toward the group? Ideally seating is close enough to reach out and hold hands in a circle.
- Do your multimedia rooms provide adequate seating to allow each person a comfortable and clear view of the screen?
- Are quiet zones quiet even with other activity in the house?
- Are sleeping areas designed for true rest or are they cluttered, busied with the call of work or unfinished tasks? Your sleeping area should be a quiet place that lures you in to relaxing sleep & rest. If you read before you fall out to sleep, have a place for one book, two at the most. One might be the

Bible and the other a current text or novel you are reading. Place a soft light reading lamp within easy reach from your bed. Remove the clutter of books and make a commitment to one book until it is done. If you do need other choices of reading material near your bed, such as children's books, have a small shelf near the bed just for current books you are completing... don't try to sleep with every book you own in your room.

· If this area is shared with a home office or other activity in your room, make a clear distinction between that activity and your sleeping space.

AFFIRMATIONS:
- I have a balance of activity, conversation, and quiet areas in my home.
- I have a balance of activity, conversation, and quiet areas outside of my home.

30 DAY PROJECT REVIEW QUESTIONS:
1. What is your current system to create and organize activity spaces?
2. What about your current activity spaces is working?
3. What improvements would you like to make to your activity spaces?
4. List the goals you have for this area in your HMN.
5. Choose one or two priority goals from this area you can accomplish or get started on this week. Write them in your Home Management Notebook.

TOOLKIT:
- Activity Balance Wheel, Form 22-1

SUGGESTIONS FOR FUTHER STUDY:
- *Breathe: Creating Space for God in a Hectic Life* by Keri Wyatt Kent

Day Twenty-Three
HOME SECURITY

"And lead us not into temptation, but deliver us from the evil one."
Matthew 6: 13

The most embarrassing parenting moments, always happen at the most inappropriate places. This was certainly the case when I discovered in the church lobby that one of my children had been checking out some inappropriate sites on the internet. I was setting up my laptop computer at our Military Outreach booth in the church lobby to run a digital video a soldier had sent us from his duty in Iraq. I also had double duty that morning as our worship team's projectionist. Arriving a little behind schedule, as commonly happens when you try to get kids up and to church early, I had to ask my team member to finish setting up the video on my computer while I ran in to prepare the projection for the morning service. Everything worked out on time and the soldier's video was running on my computer in the lobby when I took a short break between sets.

While I was shutting down the projection booth after the service, my team member came up to me and informed me that some interesting things appeared on my computer while she was trying to get Windows Media Player to work. She tactfully described the messages that rolled across the title screens as they opened up the program. It was evident that someone had gone to some extremely inappropriate sites and had not covered their tracks very well. I assured her that I was not spending my weekends looking at pornographic material but that I would need to investigate and find out which one of my children had been. Luckily, she informed me, no one else had witnessed the descriptive title screens and no images were available.

After some investigation I determined that this was not the only link on the player and so my child's excuse that it was an accident was not holding up. I am sure many of you have dealt with something similar on the internet. Possibly your children are going to sites you don't feel are uplifting or go against your values. Even worse, your children may be involved in chat rooms that can lead to dangerous encounters when they offer too much information to criminals on the other end pretending to be someone else. These are real dangers and things that need to be evaluated as you inventory your Home Security.

I am focusing on home technology security because this is new territory for many of us. Many of our kids are more computer savvy than we are so it is often difficult to protect them if they are insistent about getting involved with these temptations on the internet. The internet is an invaluable tool for school and your child's community and yet, a very vulnerable area for spiritual, physical, and mental assault.

In addition to dangers to our children, you could be receiving spam or a virus and need to protect your data and personal information from hackers. This section is meant to get you thinking about the type of protections you will need. It is not meant to be an inclusive source for protecting your computer. Get information about parental controls, privacy, security, and passwords to help monitor the use of the internet and the computer from computer technicians in your area. You can put a password on your boot-up bios to keep the kids off the computer when you're not home. With more advanced operating systems, you can assign a password to each individual and limit their time on the computer with parental controls. Individual log-ons also let you monitor your child's activity individually.

Keeping up with today's technology and deciding what is best for you family can seem overwhelming but you have to do whatever it takes to keep your family safe even if it means unplugging and taking them to the library instead. Although be careful there too because many libraries, in the name of freedom of information, do not filter their internet services and the same dangers face children online at the library. If you are not comfortable giving your kids permission to use the internet at the library, have them use your card only when you are there to watch them. Because my kids learned to hack most of the password protections by going to library and looking up hack codes, our family computer is now located on a table in the master bedroom. They are limited to an hour a day when I feel like being in my room watching them. It has just proved to be too big of a temptation for them to resist and the tempters are heartless and target the sites that kids would innocently be. So my philosophy has changed to "Lead them not into

Temptation" to the best of my ability. Keep the computer in a place where public viewing of the monitor screen is available at all times.

Another part of Home Technology is keeping your data safe from corruption. Hard-drives crash or if you do get a virus you will have to reload your operating system and start from scratch. So you need a place, an external hard-drive or usb drives, to keep a copy of your data and a place to keep your programs safe so they can be reinstalled. You'll need a back up routine that you stick to so that should you lose your hard-drive you won't lose more data than you can restore. You can use a flash-drive to keep day to day copies of things you are working on, like an article or your checkbook. And then periodically save your whole drive including digital photos to a backup hard-drive. I save mine once a month but I always have two copies of digital photos, one on my hard-drive and one in camera, or one on my hard-drive and one on my external backup hard-drive. I also burn a copy of my digital photos and finished book drafts onto two compact discs. One disc is stored in my disc storage kept in my office and the other is in my disc storage case that I keep off the premises at a family member's home. If your comfortably with storing your data online you can use iCloud Technology.

It is important to determine what computer maintenance programs are important for your computer hardware. When most hard-drives were less than a gigabyte, it was important to run routines such as scandisk and defrag to keep from running out of space. On larger hard-drives that may not seem as important but you'll still want to run them to keep your computer from slowing down. You will also need to run a virus checker, delete your temporary files and internet histories, and run your backup programs. Put these routines on your scheduler or if possible, have your computer run them automatically when you boot up or shut down.

Other multi-media that need protection are CD's, DVD's, and all those precious digital photographs. When you make a CD of your digital images, again, I suggest you make two and take a box with your name on it over to your sister's house or another family member. What a great way to ensure you have your digital images for a lifetime if something happens to your house. Another way to preserve your images is through online storage offered by many servers like Shutterfly, google, or Apple. However, the longevity of the images online is up to the company that offers the service. The advantage of online storage is accessibility; you can give friends and family links and passwords to share your images with people anywhere in the world. Be aware that storing images on social media sites like facebook, degrade your images which is fine for online use but the resolution will most likely be too small to use for print.

You can include in your "offsite" box copies of tax files and other digital data you would like to keep if something happened to your home. You can also store these in a safe deposit box if you have one large enough. It could be expensive though if you collect a lot of CD's. Make sure you offer your family member or friend the return favor of storing their cases of back up CD's and make your storage container neat and functional. A good locking CD case can hold a hundred or more CDs and would be able to be kept neatly tucked away in a closet or storage space.

This is also a good time to evaluate the rest of your home security including physical security, protecting your material wealth, and lowering the risk of identity theft.

AFFIRMATIONS:
- ☐ I have protected my family from harmful internet and televised threats.
- ☐ I have a backup routine that adequately protects our digital valuables.
- ☐ I have provided adequate home security, physical and materially, for my family and home.

30 DAY PROJECT REVIEW QUESTIONS:
1. What is your current home security system?
2. What about your current home security system is working/
3. What improvements need to be made to your system of home security?
4. List your goals in this area in your HMN.
5. Choose one or two priorities goals you can accomplish or get started on this week. Write these in your HMN.

TOOL KIT:
- ➢ Computer access protection.
- ➢ Computer security programs.
- ➢ Data backup routines and storage systems.
- ➢ Home Security Systems.
- ➢ Identity Theft Protection.

SUGGESTIONS FOR FURTHER STUDY:

- ➤ *Internet Survival Guide: Protecting Your Home Computer* by James Christiansen
- ➤ *The Complete Book of Home, Site and Office Security* by Bill Phillips

Day Twenty-Four
OUTSOURCING

"Plans fail for lack of counsel, but with many advisers they succeed."
Proverbs 15:22

"Do not hold back the wages of a hired man overnight."
Leviticus 19:13

It wasn't a big drip so who is going to notice, right? I don't have to tell you that little drips become big problems, do I? Probably not, I am a die-hard do it yourselfer. I have a hard time paying anyone for something I could do myself whether it is scrubbing the tub or fixing the toilet. My husband and I even repaired the hot-water heater together. That saved us hundreds of dollars and was very satisfying. However, we had this one little problem we could not seem to solve. The little drip that magically appeared in the garage after the kids took a shower.

The funny thing about the little drip is it only seemed to drip when one of our four children took a shower or bath. We assumed that he must have been letting water get onto the floor. So we began instructing him on the bathroom etiquette he must have missed somewhere along the way. With four children, it is not uncommon to find out that a child has missed a lesson or two along the way. I put down a bigger bath mat and even towels to ensure his mistakes would not end up in the garage during his learning period. However, the drip continued and now it was getting bigger.

After about six months of trying to track the drip, a little mold was beginning to appear in the ceiling under the bathtub. We decided to take action and called in a plumber. Of course, he did his test: shower on, tub plugged, no leak; shower off, faucet on, tub plugged, no leak; drain tub, no leak. We were perplexed to find out that seventy dollars later we had no leak. However, the plumber recommended we reseal along the floor and we complied.

The little drip continued whenever this particular child took a shower and by now quite a large puddle appeared in the garage. A friend of mine offered to look at the problem. He discovered a small drip around the edge of the tub behind the wall. He suggested we recaulk along the rim of the tub again and we compiled. Although I was skeptical for awhile, it actually seemed to work.

Then one day after my son showered I walked through the garage and heard a drip. I ran upstairs expecting to find the bathroom floor wet but it was not. I pulled everything out of the closet and saw the little drip that my friend had seen three months ago. I followed it the best I could back to the source. It did seem to be coming from the edge of the tub but we had caulked that. Standing in front of the showerhead fully clothed, I contemplated. What does this child do that no one else does? I realized he had left the shower switch in the on position and shut off the water using the hot and cold water handles individually without turning off the shower. The other children shut off the shower first. Then I heard the first clue to solving the mystery one big drip in the tub.

We knew the tub did not leak and the drain did not leak and the pipes were not leaking so I got down and looked more closely at the faucet and it was leaking. Now a faucet leaking should just drip into the tub and go down the drain but this was different. Because he had left the shower diverter open there was not enough pressure to form a true drip that would fall into the tub. Instead the drip flowed back up the underside of the faucet. Then it traveled back along the underside of the faucet to meet the pipe. It followed the pipe back into the wall, then found a nick right were the pipe and the tub met. There it flowed under the tub and down until it beaded up and dropped down into the hole that eventually lead to the garage. Water is tricky like that.

Now, you may think that the moral of this story is to do more yourself since we had three other people trying to figure this out for us for over a year, while we watched the mold grow and the ceiling cave in. But my point is only that you know your home better than anyone else you hire and you need to gather as much evidence as you can before you hire out the work and/or do it yourself.

I called our handy man and said, "This is what I found out can you fix it." He said, "Yes the faucet washers are probably bad you can do that yourself." And he told me everything I needed to do to fix the problem. Plumbers are very helpful like that; They don't need your job they are over booked as it is.

What you need to know is when to do it yourself and when to get help? And whether you hire it out or do it yourself keep track of the symptoms and repairs because that is what will help you solve the problem next time around.

One day my hot water went out and I remembered once that my husband had reset a circuit breaker button that I thought was on the hot water heater itself. But I could not find it. I checked the circuit breaker box and that circuit breaker was good. So I remembered the drip and the last time we had to drain the hot water heater to repair it and I determined under my current circumstances to hire out right away. I watched the plumber come in, remove a gray panel, push a red button, and write me out a bill for sixty-five dollars. I said, "I was looking for that button." And he politely showed me again where it was and said, "Yea. Check to make this little red button isn't tripped before you call. You could save a trip charge and just reset it yourself." No kidding.

There are a lot of reasons to call someone out. Maybe you don't have the expertise or the time or you don't have the specialized tools needed. Those are all good reasons to hire out the project but pay attention when they come out. There are just as many reasons not to hire out . Watch and learn. I would never call out the plumber to push that red button again.

Another thing to remember about hiring help is to call around and get references. Keep a log of who you do hire, how much they charged, and what they did for you. Also make a note about their service. Eventually, you will establish a relationship with an individual (my preference) or company that you know you can trust and recommend to your friends. Having a handyman is a great idea to. This person will either do the work for you or let you know who to call. Handymen are very busy so having a handyman you trust who is familiar with your home is a great asset. They will often give you advice so you can do it yourself, or you can hire them to swing by and give you some advice to get you started and to be called in if you get in a jam. Plus since they are usually not licensed in any one particular area they are less expensive. But realize that if they charge by the hour they may end up charging more because they often take longer. My plumber is so quick if I don't keep track he is gone before I even realize he is there. He charges by the hour but I've never seen him in my home more than 15 minutes. He knows his area of expertise and does a great job quickly. No chit chat.

Beware of the chitchat. I was being polite to the field tractor repair guy who came out to the ranch to work on my tractor. We started talking about tractors and farms and though he only did about five minutes' worth of work on the tractor he charged me for an hour and half of service that we spent talking. Always get the job over, get your price, and then let them talk while you write the check.

You can get references from your friends, family, neighbors, and those you work with. You can also get helpful how to information at the hardware store. I went into the hardware store to buy a new garbage disposal and after going over the different models to choose from, the clerk suggested I pull it out and bring it in. But before I pull it, he said to take an Allen wrench and turn the crank at the bottom to make sure I get all the water out. Sometimes he said, "that will even fix the problem." Sure enough, a couple cranks with the Allen wrench and the disposal started working again just fine. You don't have to do it alone to do-it-yourself.

Some Suggestions About Contracting Out
⇒ Get help when needed.
⇒ Get the right help. Determine what you can do yourself and exactly what you want the hired help to do for you.
⇒ Get recommendations from friends and family before you call.
⇒ Keep track of your references for future use by maintaining a maintenance log including who fixed it, you or an outside resource, if you were satisfied with the work, what the costs were of parts and labor, the symptoms and the fix.

Another part of outsourcing is the giving and receiving of labor. A great way to spend a weekend with your friends is what I call a "Rally Round the House" group. You and your friends spend one weekend a month at each other's home working on busting down their to-do list. You each make a to-do list of what you would like done and prioritize it. Then pull from the list the items you would trust your friends with doing. They look at your list and determine what skills they have to offer or would be willing to learn from you. You do the same with their lists and you plan to spend a Friday night or Saturday together at your house one weekend and at their house the next weekend. Of course if you have four families involved you can rally at someone's house every weekend. Our group is pretty flexible and we will complete a project at one house before we move on to the next. It's a great way to socialize and give into each other's lives in practical ways.

AFFIRMATIONS:

- ☐ I have a maintenance log that includes all repairs I have done and have had done in my home.
- ☐ I have an outsourcing resource list that includes contact information, type of services offered, jobs they have done for me or my friends, and recommendations about the service received.
- ☐ I have at least one other person or family that I exchange home repair or improvement projects with.

30 DAY PROJECT REVIEW QUESTIONS:

1. What is your current system of outsourcing?
2. What about your current outsourcing system works?
3. What about your outsourcing system needs improvement?
4. List your goals in this area in your HMN.
5. Choose one or two priority goals in this area that you can accomplish or get started on this week. Write them in your HMN.

TOOLKIT:

- ➢ Maintenance Log
- ➢ Resource List

SUGGESTIONS FOR FURTHER STUDY:

- ➢ *Don't Sweat it... Hire It!: An A to Z Guide to Finding, Hiring & Managing Home Improvement Pros* by Phil Schmidt

Day Twenty-five
RELATIONSHIPS

"First go and be reconciled to your brother; then come and offer your gift."

I have a very wise friend. One day I was complaining to her about how my mother never just called me to say, "Hello," and she replied, "How often do you call her just to say 'Hello'."

"Well every time she calls me someone has died or is sick or something. It's like she calls me out of duty."

My friend replied, "How often do you call your mom just to say 'Hello?"

I tried to explain to her that I wanted a closer relationship with my mom other than her sense of duty to inform me of people dying.

She looked at me, shook her head, and then explained it to me.

"That is what is happening in your mother's life. She is getting older and more of the people close to her are dying. She thinks you and she have these people in common and it gives her something to talk to you about so she thinks it might be important to you so she calls to tell you. What do you pick up the phone to call her about?"

"Well, I don't really call unless something is happening either." I admitted.

"If you want to change the dynamics of the relationship, you are going to have to start with you, not her." She told me if I wanted my mother to call just to chat I would have to start by calling her just to chat. If I wanted my friends to stop in unannounced more often to just say "Hi", I would have to stop in unannounced more often to just say "Hi." I wasn't so sure they wanted me to stop in unannounced and say, "Hi" but she explained that I wouldn't know until I tried.

Another time, I was talking with a woman who was upset because her husband didn't love her enough or appreciate the things she did for him enough. She said she made fancy dinners for him after work and all he wanted to do was go to bed. She tried to make plans for them to spend more time together on the weekends but he made plans to spend time hunting or playing golf with his guy-friends. The more we talked about it, it became evident that the plans she was making were really about how much more her husband could love her and not how she could love her husband better. I suggested she started by asking her husband directly, "How can I love you better?" I asked her to trust that real love never returns void.

It takes time to have relationships. To pick up the phone and call, to stop by, to get to know the needs of others and we are all called by God to love one another. So this should be a priority in our lives. Often we lose track of friends, don't even know our neighbors, and only see our church family on Sunday mornings because we are just too busy. At funerals every-one vows not to let another friend die without them knowing we love them. But soon we slip back into our same old patterns of busyness. If something is important, you must schedule it into your day planner.

So start right now by writing down twelve of the most important relationships in your life, such as::

1. God
2. My Spouse
3. My children
4. My parents
5. My siblings
6. My friends
7. My church family
8. My extended family
9. My neighbors
10. My community & city
11. My State
12. My Country

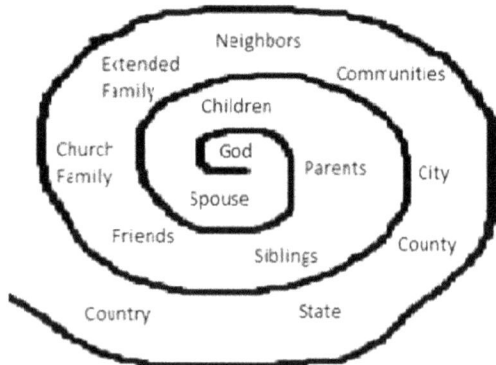

From the above list, you can list actual names of people and rela-tionships that are important enough in your life to make time for. The idea is that God is the center of your life and your inner circle is where you devote the most intense quality and quantity in a relationship. These twelve spheres move out like a spiral and as you move out from the inner circle the intensity drops off.

The above list is just a sample. Your list may vary in accordance with God's calling on your life. Don't let it be so complicated that you miss forming relationships with the people the Holy Spirit is drawing near to you. This tool kit is to encourage you think about the order of priority you put your relationships in and then evaluate the time and energy you devote to each relationship. Do your priorities add up? Do you need to make some changes? Is God really in your inner circle? Pray about what changes and adjustments you need to make to balance time with family, friends, and fellowship while loving your neighbor, honoring your parents, and training up your children.

Are there people God has brought into your life that should be included on your spiral? Do you avoid them because they don't fit into your schedule conveniently? Evaluate where you are spending a lot of energy and time at the expense of another. A good example of this is parents of newborns who begin to neglect their marriage relationship because they get busy and worn out by the kids. The marriage came first and it should be given its rightful place on your schedule. Taking the time to keep this relationship healthy will supply the energy reserves you need to avoid being burned out by the kids.

In creating spaces I mentioned my friend who designed a quiet sitting room in her master bedroom. It consists of a recliner for her, a recliner for him, and a table with a reading lamp between them. It is a natural draw for each of them to find a place of peace in the midst of the storm of raising five kids. Often, at least daily, she and her husband would find themselves there together for quiet conversations, reading, and praying together.

We love because He first loved us. We can't get anything out of a relationship until we take the time to feed into it. Design ways to ensure you don't neglect the important relationships in this life starting with your personal relationship with God. It is the love from this relationship that will feed into the next relationship on the circle and energize it. The love of a good marriage feeds into a loving relationship with the kids. The kids loving relationship with their parents will feed into their relationships with their peers. And it just moves out.

When relationships on the outer-most rings get out of sorts, pull back to the inner rings for support. The center of your support is always God. When relationships get tested, take it to God in prayer and let him led you back out along the spiral to set the relationships right again.

The best book to read about developing good relationships is the bible. There is so much in there that I can not even begin to capture it all. I just want to highlight a couple truths that will help you right your relationships but first of all I want to point you to the source, the Good News. You will find all you need to know about righting your relationships in the scriptures of the New Testament which teach us how to live with one another.

One of those truths is called forgiveness. I could talk all day about the good news of forgiveness. We were forgiven and that is good news but we are also blessed by forgiving others. That is where the power of forgiveness lies for our lives here are on earth. When you don't forgive, a bitter root grows in you no the one you refuse to forgive. Always take this to the Lord in prayer but a helpful way to learn this is to follow simple strategies from scripture;

Steps To Reconciliation

1. Be reconciled by taking your offense directly to the person who offended you.
2. If they don't listen, take a witness and confront the person with your offense.
3. Forgive the person with or without reconciliation.
4. If they will not be reconciled with you, take it to the church to help you determine your next step, ensuring you've done what you can and shake the dust off and move on.
5. True forgiveness means giving the person's transgressions against you to God to deal with. The goal is to be reconciled and often you will find in step one that it was just a misunderstanding. By bringing it out into the open you can come to an understanding. However, it is important that if you cannot come to reconciliation that you do not harbor an offense in your heart where it can manifest ill will and permeate into your other relationships by developing roots of mistrust and bitterness.

"What is bound on earth, will be bound in heaven. What is loosed on earth, will be loosed in heaven."

AFFIRMATIONS:

- ☐ I have prioritized my twelve circles of relationships and have evaluated how I am spending my time in each one and have prayerfully created balance among them.
- ☐ I have prayed that the Holy Spirit reveal any un-forgiveness I have toward others and have worked to reconcile it.
- ☐ I have scheduled time for the most important relationships in my life.
- ☐ I follow the example of my First Relationship, my relationship with God who loved me first, by loving others without waiting to be loved first.

30 DAY PROJECT REVIEW QUESTIONS:

1. What is your current system of managing relationships?
2. What about your current devotion to relationships is working?
3. What about your relationships need improvement?
4. List your goals in this area in your HMN.
5. Choose one or two priority goals in this area that you can accomplish or get started on this week. Write them in your HMN.

TOOLKIT:

- ➤ Circle of Relationships
- ➤ Steps to Reconciliation

SUGGESTIONS FOR FURTHER STUDY:

- ➤ *Total Forgiveness* by R. T. Kendall
- ➤ *The Heart of the Five Love Languages* by Gary Chapman

Day Twenty-Six
PRACTICING GIFTS

"God has given each of us the ability to do certain things well. So if God has given you the ability to prophesy, speak out when you have faith that God is speaking through you. If your gift is that of serving others, serve them well. If you are a teacher, do a good job of teaching. If your gift is to encourage others, do it! If you have money, share it generously. If God has given you leadership ability, take the responsibility seriously. And if you have a gift for showing kindness to others, do it gladly."

Romans 12:6-8 (NLT)

"I got to play the piano!" My favorite part of this Christmas celebration was that I got to play the piano for our family's Christmas carols singalong. Secretly I had hoped that I would but I didn't really expect it. I didn't even expect to have the family come together and sing. It's not an annual thing but once or twice over the years it has happened. Normally, the guitar players lead the group. This year the piano was next to the tree and invited the want-to-be piano players to take a try at it. Each sitting down in due time and playing a short demo of their small samples of songs they have committed to memory. Then as the tables were cleared and the crowd gathered around the Christmas tree for the annual gift exchange, someone offered that someone else could play for the singing of Christmas carols but they declined. And one by one the want-to-be players all dismissed themselves from the side of the room with the piano. Being the owner of the piano, someone suggested that I play. "I'll do the best I can." I said feeling confident no one else thought they could do better and everyone was very gracious for all my mistakes and seemed thrilled with the less than perfect accompaniment I provided.

What an awesome moment in my life to be able to use my developing gift to praise God with my family. With much more practice I may be able to play for a less forgiving crowd. God has given us each gifts with all intentions that we share them with his people. However, that does not eliminate the need to develop the gifts through long hours of practice on our own.

I have always known I loved to play piano. Even though, I have not spent a lot of time developing my talent. My late husband was a guitar player and that was his passion. He played every day and he pursued a career in music and that is also how we entertained ourselves on the weekends. He was all music, all the time. I however love music and dance and horses and sports and writing and school and counseling and electronics and technology and a number of other pursuits that distracted me from piano playing.

Having a wide variety of interests isn't all bad if you realize that you won't be really good at anyone thing. But the best part of participating in many things is to discover those that you really do enjoy. Somewhere among them you will notice that certain things seem to come easier for you and others are a constant struggle to the point of total frustration. I believe that God has given us some underlying talents and with practice they can be developed into a useable gift. The areas you enjoy and can't understand why people think they are so hard are more than likely the areas of your gifts.

GETTING STARTED:

How do you know what your gifts are? There are a lot of interest and talent surveys you can take to help you narrow down your gifts but I think the best way to find out is to take a look at the things you do. What do you do well, what do you love, where are your thoughts when you aren't doing what you should be doing? Sometimes we think we want to be something because we enjoy watching others doing it or intellectually we think that would be interesting. But then actually doing it, we discover it isn't as enjoyable. I believe there is a joy in our gifts and without joy we are probably in the wrong area. It doesn't mean it will be absolutely easy or without frustrating moments as the talent in that gifting develops. But generally you should realize that it comes much easier than other things, you stick with it more, and people seem to be amazed at how natural it is for you.

Another way to discover your gifts is to think about an event or trial when you were successful. Detail the event as it unfolded. Then think about what you did to make it or contributed to the event being a success or overcoming the trial. What kind of talent, skill, or gifting did it take? Think about other events or trials and catalog the skills and talents you have drawn on in the past to succeed. Soon you will begin to see a pattern and begin to develop a better understanding of your own gifts. Remind yourself of these talents and skills as you face challenges in your life. You have used them in the past and you can use them in the future.

In your home, your family members should be allowed to explore, discover, and practice their gifts. Sometimes it is frustrating for other family members because no one wants to be inundated with the screech of a budding violinist or the heart pounding bongs of a new drummer. As room and space allow, try to designate a place for creative arts and talents. Also provide plenty of opportunities to let family members show off their developing talents with non-critical audiences such as your family and your extended family and friends. Then as their talents develop make sure they have opportunities to move out into other venues such as a school play or drama team or musical group. Remember that gifts and talents are not all in the form of creative arts.

Learn to see beyond what our culture claims are successful talents. Those talents are often limited to academic, fine arts, or sports achievements. Success comes in many forms such as compassion, being able to

1 Corinthians 12:1-14	1 Corinthians 12:27-30	Romans 12:6-8	Ephesians 4:11
Wisdom	Apostleship	Prophecy	Apostleship
Knowledge	Prophecy	Ministry	Prophecy
Discerning of spirits	Teaching	Teaching	Evangelism
Prophecy	Working of miracles	Exhortation	Pastoring
Speaking in tongues	Healing	Giving	Teaching
Interpretation of tongues	Helps	Leading	
Faith	Administration	Showing mercy (compassion)	
	Speaking in tongues		
Working of miracles			
Healing			

work with your hands, strong labor, fixing things, working with wood, managing a home, understanding children, or being a willing follower. There are as many possible and unique talents and gifts as there are humans. The Old Testament boasts of many talents such as craftsmanship, playing musical instruments, writing poems, having great faith, and interpreting dreams. The important thing is to not compare your gifts and talents or those of your spouse or children to those of others. "They are all gifts from God so no one should boast." As scripture also points out, "There are different kinds of gifts, but the same Spirit. There are different kinds of service, but the same Lord. There are different kinds of working, but the same God works all of them in all men (1 Corinthians 12:4-6)."

Do you appreciate the unique gifts and talents of others? Recognize and compliment gifts when you see them. Many hidden heroes go behind the scenes of any production, church service, or even a family meal. Let them know you recognize their efforts.

AFFIRMATIONS:
- ☐ I know and continue to development my God given gifts and talents.
- ☐ I offer plenty of opportunities for my family members to explore and development their God given gifts and talents.
- ☐ I recognize the gifts and talents of others and acknowledge their contributions with gratitude.

30 DAY PROJECT REVIEW QUESTIONS:
1. What is your current system for practicing gifts?
2. What about your current system for practicing gifts is working well?
3. What improvements need to made to the way you practice gifts in your home?
4. List your goals for this area in your HMN.
5. Choose one or two priority goals in this area to accomplish or get started on this week. Write them down in your HMN.

TOOLKIT:
- ➤ Gifts and Talents Tables
- ➤ Interests and Personality Inventories

SUGGESTIONS FOR FURTHER STUDY:
- ➤ *Larry Burkett's All About Talent: Discovering Your Gifts and Personality* by Larry Burkett

- ➢ *Discovering Your Spiritual Gifts: A Personal Inventory Method* by Dr. Kenneth C. Kinghorn
- ➢ *What Color is Your Parachute?* by Richard Nelson Bolles

Day Twenty-seven
HOSPITALITY

"Offering hospitality is a way to love each other deeply which covers over a multitude of sins"

1 Peter 4:8-9 NIV

I have never felt so much at home as at my sister's house. My husband and I and my first born son squeezed into one of her smaller houses during a transition period of our lives. I have always wanted a home like my sister's, where people are comfortable dropping in at any time. She has always been very welcoming. Over the years she has offered many people a place to live .

I have always wanted a home like my first Christian mentors, Nick and Ineke. Their home is so warm and welcoming and they had the knack of making you feel very special. After Ineke died, I found out that a lot of people felt the very same way. She made you feel as if you were the most important person in the world to her. Ineke was a great hostess and I so enjoyed being invited into her home especially the time she invited my husband and I to an intimate dinner with just her and Nick.

My mother put a passion of hosting in my heart at an early age by having Danish dinners and fondue parties with larger gatherings of her close friends. She fueled that passion by starting my China dish collection when I was sixteen. I began using the china plates and serving dishes with my family at Christmas dinners. However, our family has grown so large that it doesn't have the intimacy of the sit down dinners I love to host with six or eight people. These smaller dinners seem more hospitable because they encourage a more casual, intimate conversation with each of your guests.

Hospitality is more than just fixing food and cleaning your house up to show it off. It is about creating an environment that is favorable to the growth and development of your relationships to each other and to God.

We are called to love one another. It is hard to love someone you don't spend any time with or hardly know. Opening your home up for hospitality means getting to know others and letting them get to know you in your most intimate place, your home. This happens when people start dropping in unannounced. They get to see the real you not the fixed up for company you. The more time you spend with others in your home and in theirs, the more deeply you can love them.

Scriptures call us to show Hospitality for the following reasons:
1. Showing Hospitality is a good deed (1 Tim 5:10)
2. Offering Hospitality is a way to love each other deeply which covers over a multitude of sins (1 Peter 4:8-9)
3. Showing Hospitality is a way to work together for the truth (3 John 1:8)

When you open your home to others you can help ease their burdens, by giving them something to eat, someone to hear them, someone to notice their lives, and by praying with them and developing a deeper friendship. Romans 12:12-13 sums it up as this: "Be joyful in hope, patient in affliction, faithful in prayer. Share with God's people who are in need. Practice hospitality." This is more than just an evening dinner with friends around your dining room table, not that you can't start there. But I believe God is calling us to be even more generous with our homes.

Mike Jentes describes hospitality in his online article, *My House and Hospitality,* as "letting others be at home in your home." Now that reminds me of the time I went back to my parents house after living on my own for period of time. I was thinking about going into the kitchen and getting a drink and wondered, "Hmmm... am I welcome to help myself or have things changed now that I don't reside here?" I asked my mom for drink and she fixed me one. It still felt odd as if I was too lazy to get it myself, yet, I thought I was actually being polite by not helping myself. When an older sibling came over and helped himself to the fridge and even ate her food, I wondered why I didn't feel more at home in my parents' house.

Helping yourself is truly a feeling of being at home where you are. Feeling at home in someone else's house is a process of intimacy. You don't just help yourself to the fridge of a friend on your first visit to their house. It takes time to develop that kind of a relationship. Your friend tells you to "help yourself" or "please look for that in the fridge." And after becoming accustomed to being told to help yourself you develop a level of intimacy that means you can as a general rule help yourself.

Jentes wasn't just talking about the refrigerator. He is talking about a whole new level of Hospitality. A level of hospitality that means we no longer think of our houses as our homes but as God's homes for those who the Holy Spirit draws into our lives. More than just being cordial, hospitality means being generous with all that we own. If our house belongs to God then it belongs to all his children and we are just maintaining it for their use. Welcoming, with genuine love and hospitality, those God opportunities that knock on your door when you least expect it is what we are called to do.

GETTING STARTED:

You have taken one of the biggest steps of getting started if you have made it this far in the 30-Day project. You are in the process of "Making Ready Your Home" for God opportunities when they knock at the door. Don't wait until your home is perfect to invite others in to meet the real you and relax, we are all a work in progress.

Start inviting people into your home regularly whether they accept the invitation or not. Don't give up. It took my dear friend over a year to get me to step out of my comfort zone and attend a small group meeting at her home. She never gave up asking me and it turned out to be one of the biggest breakthroughs that helped me out of the hermit-style social pattern I'd developed over the years that had begun to isolate me from others. Keep asking.

Invite a neighbor over for a cup of coffee or tea on the deck or around the kitchen table. This is a great way to find out who they are and begin a relationship. If someone knocks at your door invite them in to sit at your kitchen table and have a glass of iced tea or lemonade. I love offering a little conversation break to the plumber or electrician, just make sure they are off the clock before they sit down and drink their lemonade.

Prepare a guestroom and be prepared to invite someone to stay in your home when the need arises. You'll be surprised how God will use this one before you even know it. You don't have to have entire room available. Purchase an inflatable bed and have a set of sheets ready to offer up a place to stay.

There are many creative ways to start using your home for hospitality including hosting a small group or cell group in your home, having a "girlfriends" slumber party (of course this idea is for the ladies), or ask a discouraged friend to stay over. Start a monthly game night or movie night at your house. These are great ways to regularly check in with friends you might not otherwise see for months or years and to invite new friends into your group.

Some questions to ask yourself:

1. How are you practicing hospitality in your home?
2. Are you sharing God's love and the Good news to the lost in your home?
3. Could you do more to honor your parents in your home?
4. Are you using your home to minister to the Kingdom of believers?
5. Are you using your home to build relationship with your adult children and grandchildren?
6. Have your neighbors ever been invited into your home?
7. Who does your home serve?

As a child, I always felt honored when my mother invited me to her weekly coffee with the neighbor ladies. I was introduced, allowed to sit with the adults, and doted over as the ladies chatted and conducted the business of the neighborhood. Our neighborhood was very close, like family, and I believe "coffee" was the reason. Weekly "coffee" group rotated from one home to another and included an update on their lives, neighborhood party and picnic planning, and dessert. The extension of the neighborhood coffee clutch was a monthly game of bingo. Each lady brought a gift and each went home with a gift. The idea wasn't to win at bingo but rather to talk and laugh and keep each other up to date on the kids and latest news. Still in their seventies, the bingo game goes on and they are still talking about us kids.

Hospitality is, as the scripture tells us, a way to open up your home to others and build up relationships. There is something about bringing others into your private residence that deepens the relationship more than meeting them anywhere else. As you begin to think of your home as belonging to God, letting others be at home in your home, and loosening your grips of personal ownership, the doors of opportunity to practice hospitality will open and your whole lifestyle will change.

AFFIRMATIONS:

☐ When someone knocks, I let them in (with security precautions considered).

- ☐ I am prepared to share a drink with a stranger, a meal with a neighbor, or offer a discouraged friend a place to sleep.
- ☐ I regularly use my home to minister to, encourage, and connect with others.
- ☐ I understand the idea that my home belongs to God and that I am only the steward assigned to offer it up to encourage and serve others.

30 DAY PROJECT REVIEW QUESTIONS:

1. What is your current system for practicing Hospitality?
2. What about your current system for Hospitality is working well?
3. What improvements need to be made to the way you practice Hospitality in your home?
4. List your goals for this area in your HMN.
5. Choose one or two priority goals in this area to accomplish or get started on this week. Write them down in your HMN.

TOOLKIT:

- ➤ Provisions for guests.
- ➤ Hospitality Planner

SUGGESTIONS FOR FURTHER STUDY

- ➤ *Practicing Hospitality: The Joy of Serving Others* by Patricia A. Ennis and Lisa Tatlock
- ➤ *Simple Hospitality* by Jane Jarrell

Day Twenty-eight
SLEEP AND REST

"The sleep of a laborer is sweet, whether he eats little or much, but the abundance of a rich man permits him no sleep."

Ecclesiastes 5:12

Sleep is an interesting quality of life. It is fascinating to think we must go unconscious on a daily basis to survive. If we do not enter what Webster defines as, "a physiological state of rest that includes relative physical and nervous inactivity, unconsciousness, and lessened responsiveness to external stimuli," then we begin to experience physical, mental, and spiritual repercussions. Lack of sleep causes what researchers call a "sleep deprivation" and possibly a "sleep debt" that needs to be repaid. According to research cited in the Wikipedia, an online encyclopedia, sleep debt is highly debated but sleep deprivation has been proven to result in blurred vision, irritability, memory lapses, overall confusion, hallucinations, nausea, increased stress hormones, slurred speech, psychosis, and in rats even premature death.

Symptoms of sleep deprivation begin when the body is not allowed to enter into a restful sleep period of somewhere between six and nine hours a night depending on the individual need. Without proper sleep there is the danger of micro-sleep, which causes one to nod off for a few seconds when engaged in repetitive activity. Another danger to depriving yourself of adequate sleep is the increase of insulin resistance which causes more stress hormone to be released and results in higher blood sugar levels (2005, April 25, Archives of Internal Medicine, 165 (8), pp 863-7). This is especially dangerous for people with diabetes but in addition some researchers believe it can cause early-stage diabetes. The Journal of Sleep contains volumes of research on sleep that correlate sleep deprivation with negative mental and physical health effects including the onset and delayed recovery of illnesses, early onset of disease, lowered pain tolerance, and an increase in behavioral and cognitive disorders.

The fact is we need sleep to remain healthy and function at our best. Even God rested and he gave us sleep as a gift. "In vain you rise early and stay up late, toiling for food to eat--- for [the Lord] grants sleep to those he loves (Psalm 127:2)." Who would want to miss the sweet sleep that God has given for him?

I think it is so interesting how God built the sleep cycle into our very being. Our bodies are in tune with an internal clock called the circadian rhythm based on a 24-hour period and most living things on this planet on are in synch with it. This body clock increases the concentration of blood sugar in humans just as the day is dawning whether you've stayed up all night or not. In a healthy human being this sets in motion other processes such as an increase in insulin to counteract the increase in sugar. The morning dawn effect is thought to awake our body and prepare us for the stress of the day. This explains why when my husband and I would drive across country without stopping I would feel exhausted about two or three hours before dawn but as the sun came up I woke up and felt as if I had slept all night. However, I experienced a lag or possibly a sleep debt in the afternoon that had to be made up with a nap.

GETTING STARTED:

Every home should have quiet places where family members can find rest and relaxation. Create as many ways to relax in your home as you can and plan to use them. I like to start in the bedrooms. I set them up with a place to relax. In my room, that consists of lots of pillows on my headboard and a recliner and reading lamp. In the morning I take a few minutes to tidy up the room, make the bed, spray a mist of air freshener, and close the door on the way out. When I finish the daily run-myself-ragged list, I can open my bedroom door to a wonderful surprise and enter into a refreshing place to rest. My son loves it when I let him open the door. He exclaims, "Look, mom, the maid was here!" I tell myself, "Forget the fact that you were the maid and just enjoy it!"

Create lots of relaxing nooks and crannies in your home like a reading corner or a two person breakfast table for reading the morning paper. I enjoy relaxing at the piano playing worship music. There is nothing like a warm, bubble bath with some soft music and a good book. We set up a corner table designated to working on puzzles. When we lost a dear friend of the family, the puzzle table became the place we each came to rest our minds from the constant mental torture this tragedy demanded of us. My grown daughter would come home to find comfort from me and not knowing what to say or do, together sitting at the puzzle table studying the shapes and colors we mourned without words.

Consider again the balance of resting places in your home in comparison to your activity centers in your home. Make sure you include resting areas outdoors as well. Take the time to enjoy both every day. You may be resting too much and need to take a break from that with a little more activity. Do you have a place where you can work out to a 20 minute aerobic tape? Is there an area in your home you can build or create things with your hands?

In addition to taking a rest break from your work or taking a work break from your rest, you need to make sure you are allowing yourself enough hours to sleep in a day. Make sure you are getting from six to nine hours of sleep a night. Talk with your doctor if you think you require more or less than this recommended amount. If you are having trouble sleeping at night, concentrate on getting up at the same time everyday whether you feel tired or not. This usually develops a need for sleep at the right time of night and levels out your body's natural rhythm. If you are napping, do the hours you nap and the hours you sleep add up to the recommended daily amount? Many experts agree that it is the daily total not the total stretch at one time that counts. Although micro-sleep does not count and can be very dangerous so keep total sleep sessions to one or two per day. Most of us don't have the luxury of napping. If you are sleeping more than ten hours, then you may just need to get up and get moving a little more. Again you can talk to your doctor about other sleep issues that may be limiting the quality of sleep you are getting.

God's Pattern for Work/Rest

1. Other than sleep itself, do you take a break from the work that you do to enter into rest throughout the day?
2. Do you make the Sabbath day Holy by setting it apart from other days?
3. Do you give you, your family members, and your animals a day of rest from their work?
4. Are you and your family members balancing work and rest throughout the day?

5. Do you follow the same 24-hour clock every day of the week, using morning and evening routines to help you?
6. Are you and your family members getting the recommended 6-9 hours of sleep each night (children and teens need at least 9)?

In addition to developing a healthy sleep routine, we need to consider our need for rest. Different from sleep where we lose all consciousness, rest is ceasing from our work and being refreshed. It's a given, God rested on the seventh day to reflect on his work finding it was good. We are commanded to observe a Sabbath day of rest for our own benefit, our own day of refreshing. Trying to work in a few extra hours on a project while the Lord is resting, is futile. "Unless the Lord builds the house, its builders labor in vain (Psalm 127:1)."

Making sure you have built in rest breaks during the day is important, as well. Jesus set the example when he directed the disciples after their long day of serving to go with him to a quiet place and rest. They were unsuccessful at that point because the crowds followed him but eventually Jesus got off alone to pray and reflect on his work. We need that down time to recharge, refresh, and to visit with God personally. Not only do we need to find ways to rest from our work but we need rest from the chatter of daily life and even from our passions. I love to write but as every writer knows you reach a point where you have to rest from it. After so many hours of writing you just get stuck, you have to walk away and let your mind rest from the activity. When you come back to it, often the creative ideas and words are flowing again.

Sometimes, rest is just that, breaking away from what we are doing and doing something totally different. If you are sitting, do something standing. If you are active, slow down. If you are analyzing, do something passive. If you are passive, do something that requires thinking. We need to learn to take the time to walk away from our indulgences like walking away from the television and seeing what life is like without the chatter. Putting the To-Do list on hold and entering into God's resting place to be refreshed.

However, you do have to be doing some work to rest from it.

"We did this, not because we do not have the right to such help, but in order to make ourselves a model for you to follow. For even when we were with you, we gave you this rule: "If a man will not work, he shall not

eat." We hear that some among you are idle. They are not busy; they are busybodies. ." 2 Thessalonians 3:9-11 (NIV)

God set the example for our work. He made a plan to create the world in a week. He broke it down into tasks that he wanted to complete each day. So the first day he went to work and after he finished the first tasks, he paused and saw that his work was good. He took a short rest. Then he moved on to the next task and when he had finished all that he planned for that day, he said, "That was good," and then he let evening pass and morning come and started again. He repeated that each day until on the six day he said, "I'm done and it's good." Then he took a whole day off. He set an example for a healthy work/rest pattern

AFFIRMATIONS:
- ☐ Each night I get a good night's sleep.
- ☐ I have many places to rest and relax in my home and I use them daily.
- ☐ I work hard and rest well. I have a healthy work/rest pattern.
- ☐ I set apart one day a week for resting, reflection, and renewing of my mind and spirit.
- ☐ I ensure my family members and even my animals have a day of rest, adequate hours of sleep, and a healthy work/rest pattern.

30 DAY PROJECT REVIEW QUESTIONS:
1. What is your current system for balancing work and rest?
2. What about your current work/rest system is working well?
3. What improvements need to be made to the way you balance work and rest in your home?
4. List your goals for this area in your HMN.
5. Choose one or two priority goals in this area to accomplish or get started on this week. Write them down in your HMN.

TOOLKIT:
- ➤ God's pattern for work and rest.

SUGGESTIONS FOR FURTHER STUDY:
- ➤ *Finding Rest When the Work Is Never Done* by Patrick Klingaman

Day Twenty-nine
MASTER PLANNING

"The wise woman builds her house, but with her own hands the foolish one tears hers down."

Proverbs 14:1

At some point most of us will see something we like at the store and think, "How can I use that in my home?" When, we all know, it is best to be home when we make our list of what we need. It could be as simple as when my sister bought a brass iron shelving unit to put over her toilet. It fit her bathroom horse theme and was on sale. It was perfect until she got it home and realized that due to her over-extending vanity cabinet the perfect, horse designed shelving unit would not fit over toilet. So the shelving unit was put out into the garage for future use if the need arose. Luckily it was on sale.

We all do it and sometimes it can be costly. Especially if you've spent thousands of dollars to build a new deck and the following summer tear it out to put in a new sunroom. We need to be better planners and diligent implementers. In other words, design a plan for the future of our homes and then use it as our blueprint as we step through the implementation of that plan. If you want a sunroom, hold off on the deck for a few years and save the money you would have spent on the deck for the sunroom. If you need some outdoor space in meantime, purchase an inexpensive canopy to get you by while you save. The canopy can be moved and used in a new location once the sunroom is built.

A master plan is a design that reflects your Home Vision Statement. It includes the spaces and needs you have identified throughout the 30 day project. It is a model of your dream home that can be broken down into stages. You create the vision one stage at a time. Use all your resources on items that move you closer to fulfilling the vision while you add value to your home. Staging helps you begin with projects you can afford today while you save for the bigger ticket items. The plan keeps you from building over the top of your dream and then having to pay to undo things that were not in the master plan.

At any point in your planning, you can bring in advisors to help you design the plan. Armed with your Home Vision statement a designer or architect can offer lots of valuable ideas and help you start putting your plan together. The upfront cost of advisors is well spent if it keeps your plans realistic and insures your plans are structurally feasible. Architects can also give you cost saving ideas you may have overlooked.

GETTING STARTED:

Start your dream home design with a review of your Home Vision statement. Consider how modifications and renovations will help you achieve your personal vision and mission statements and those of your family members.

Next step in the planning is to look at the list of major repairs you developed in an earlier chapter. Take care of any items that are unsafe or left undone will deplete the value of your home's basic structure in a short amount of time. Consider less urgent repairs by how they fit into your overall modification plans. For example, don't spend $3,000 to repair a chimney that is going to be removed when you redo the great room in three years. Seal off the fireplace for three years and put the $3000 toward another project.

Design, with architectural help as needed, your master plan. This is a drawing of what your home will look like when you are done. This includes every room on the interior and every structure and landscape area on the outside from trees to driveways. The end result may be the dream you've sketched out on graph paper or a set of prints you had professionally drafted by an architectural and/or landscape designer.

As you draw up your plan think about how your family members and guests' needs will change over the life of the plan. Make any adjustments to the master plan to include those changes. Periodically review your master plan and reconsider any changes in your Home Vision, family make-up, and guests' needs.

The next step is to prioritize your design. Develop stages in the plan and include the necessity, urgency, and financial considerations of the items to be implemented. Let's say you'd like to build a separate bedroom for your son. You have the cash to do it but then you won't be able to remodel the kitchen for several years. Do you do that first or remodel the kitchen first? If your son is thirteen, you may decide to do the bedroom first. If you wait, he may only have his own room for two years. If he is already 17 is it worth it? Will he be staying home in the new room through college or moving into the dorms? What are the plans for the room if and when he does move out? How dysfunctional is the kitchen anyway?

Make your priority list with a few justifications off to the side and then if things change you can move things around a bit. At least until after the kitchen is remodeled. So you have prioritized your list. Now it is time to build stages into your plan. If the kitchen is extremely dysfunctional, maybe you can do part of your plans in the kitchen and then start the boy's room and finish up the kitchen later. Again all things must be considered including cash on hand, future savings, and urgency of the project.

Stage one, after your urgent repairs are completed, is the highest priority projects you can afford now. Afford now means spending money you have already saved for stage one projects. A separate savings account and regular allotments should be made specifically for stage two projects. I like to separate my savings into home maintenance, stage 1 projects, and stage 2 projects. This way I am constantly replenishing the funds I need to maintain my home and can do weekend and smaller projects without jeopardizing my ability to save for the big renovations I have planned. I can see that funds are growing, do as much as I can myself and still know that one day the plan will come together without going into debt to do it. Without the savings plan you can't expect to pay cash for the project because funds will always be used on smaller projects.

Once the stage 2 savings fund is big enough to complete the first large project on your list, it's time to get started. The best place to start when you're this far is to get a bid from three or four contractors that you would consider to do the work. Check out their references and recommendations. Then you will know if you have a go ahead or need to save more money. You can also get a better idea how much of it to do yourself and what you would rather pay out. Make sure you get bids that include everything you want done. Your plan should be detailed enough to include everything especially if you had an architect help you draw it up. If a bidder leaves an item out it is difficult to compare the bids to each other. Make sure you get a bid and not an estimate. A bid is a contract and consists of what they agree to do the work for. As long as nothing is left out of the contract a bid is a fixed cost where an estimate can end up costing a lot more. A bid can be higher if more work is found to be necessary as the project proceeds, such as, if a crack in the foundation is found after old drywall is removed. Fixing the foundation would not have been in the original bid and will increase the cost of the project.

The goal of this chapter is to help you design a realistic plan and enjoy pursuing it in small steps that add value to your home and move you toward your home vision. Before you implement a major renovation seek the guidance of a general contractor or seek out more information about being your own general contractor. The Master plan helps you focus the resources you do have and keeps you from being distracted by other competition for your time and resources.

AFFIRMATIONS:
- ☐ I have a Master Plan that describes in detail the long-term vision I currently have for my home.
- ☐ Before I consider any changes or major repairs I consult my Master Plan to ensure it fits in with my goals.
- ☐ I make regular allotments to a home improvement savings plan divided into three categories: home maintenance fund, stage 1 projects fund, and stage 2 projects fund.
- ☐ I regularly review my Master plan and make appropriate revisions.

30 DAY PROJECT REVIEW QUESTIONS:
1. What is your current Master Plan?
2. What about your current Master Plan is working well?
3. What improvements need to be made to your Master Plan?
4. List your goals for this area in your HMN.
5. Choose one or two priority goals in this area to accomplish or get started on this week. Write them down in your HMN.

TOOLKIT:
- ➤ Master Plan
- ➤ Savings Account(s) Allocation Plan (Day 7)

SUGGESTIONS FOR FURTHER STUDY

➢ *The Pat Fay Method. How to Manage Your Home Remodel or New Construction Without a General Contractor to Save Serious Money* by Pat Fay

➢ *The Complete Guide to Designing Your Own Home* by Scott T. Ballard

Day Thirty
MINISTERING TO OTHERS

"Like clouds and wind without rain is a man who boasts of gifts he does not give."

Proverbs 25:14

When my husband died, I felt so much comfort from the many people who reached out to our family. We had meals coming in for weeks, people stopping by to clean our house and even do our laundry. Friends offered to come by to take the kids for the weekend. I got cards and letters for weeks from people I didn't even know. It was difficult to wean myself off of such intense love and affection. I didn't think I could ever do enough to repay their kindness. When I tried to reach out to others in similar situations I felt so inadequate until a friend of mine put into perspective what really happened. She explained how everyone just came together and did a little bit and altogether it grew into the rich, intense out-pouring of love that I received.

We are called to serve one another in our homes, our churches, and in our communities. Service is making a difference in someone else's life without expecting a reward. I could not adequately thank each person that impacted me during my time of need. In my grief I saw people coming in and out of my house, leaving trays of food, or arriving in small groups to clean and I couldn't accurately keep track of every person that had contributed to the effort. They all gave a piece of themselves in self-less service to lift us up and help carry us through our pain. Each one was doing something they knew how to do, combining the skills and abilities of each to make a big impact.

We are called to come together in service with others to make a bigger impact on the lives of others than we could make alone. We are not to serve institutions like the church, but rather we are to serve the people in these institutions. At work we are to serve the people around us while we perform the skill we are being paid to perform. At church we serve as we learn to serve better. In our neighborhoods we reach and get to know the people that live there. At our schools and communities, we take the time to serve the needs of the people we meet. There are no chance meetings but rather opportunities God puts before us to serve.

We are to make use of everything we are given whether it is our money, our time, our skills, or our homes to make a difference in other people's lives without expecting a reward in return. By our example and our good deeds, we will help other people draw closer to God in both their time of need and in their daily lives. Be involved enough in their lives to help them feel uplifted and supported. The more you are involved with others, the more opportunity you will have to serve them.

GETTING STARTED:

The best way to minister to people whether at work or at home is to be transparent with them. Don't hide your faults or your pain or your imperfect life but be honest in your struggles and how you are seeking God to give you strength and direction. A bible study teacher of mine said, "In today's culture we suffer from a disease called, 'Terminal Niceness.' It builds a wall around us and keeps us from being real with each other." That doesn't mean you should go tell all your co-workers how hard your life is but try to be honest when they ask how you are doing. If you are doing great, share what God is doing. If they are hurting, be empathetic letting your experiences of pain help you understand how they might be feeling and draw you closer to them.

We are called to uplift and encourage each other because God knew it would tear down the walls that isolate us from each other and make us feel alone in the world. Getting involved in the church is a good way to get started serving others. Church service allows you to practice your serving skills in a non-judgmental atmosphere.

If you are confused about where and how you should be serving in your fellowship, pray for God's direction. It can at times become overwhelming because there are always requests for volunteers and workers. Consider first your passions and skills. If it is not apparent where those fit in, ask your church leadership for guidance.

The goal of serving in the church is to practice skills that may seem strange to us. Eventually, we may be called to take this service outside the church walls and into a less friendly environment where God's light can shine through us into a dark world.

If you have been serving for a while and are feeling burnt out or dispassionate about your service, take a break. God does not want grumpy givers. Take a step back and rethink your service. Sometimes it is helpful to just stop it all and reevaluate. Then let the Lord lead you into an area where you can passionately serve again.

I was a crisis intervention counselor when my husband was diagnosed with small cell carcinoma, a form of lung cancer. During the stress of client calls, I had to stop myself from yelling at them for whining and complaining when their issues seemed so trivial compared to the trauma my family was facing. It didn't take long for me to realize that I needed to step down from my position. It wasn't fair for me to continue to try to serve them at a time when I was unable to have compassion for their needs.

The hardest lesson I learned at that time was allowing others to serve me. When my husband was going through his second round of chemotherapy, a group of people from our church came to our house to do yard work. It was hard for me to tell them to come on over and even harder for my husband who always felt like he should be doing it all. I held a letter in my hand from the city saying if our weeds weren't cut down and the grass wasn't cut we would be fined. I was weeping when the phone rang. It was a minister from our church asking me if he could send a crew over to the house on Saturday. My first reaction was to arrogantly tell him we didn't need help but one glance at the letter in my hand and I knew I needed to say, "Please do!"

I convinced my husband to relax and enjoy the help. I thought I was going to feel awkward and embarrassed with other people in our home doing our work but as I watched this group having so much fun whacking weeds, riding around on lawn tractors, and even cleaning our windows I relaxed. I knew they were enjoying the giving as much as we were enjoying the receiving.

Do allow others to serve you and don't let pride rob you of the joy of receiving.

Service Questionnaire:
1. How are you serving now? What do you enjoy the most about it?
2. Are you serving in an ongoing position?

3. In what ways do you serve others spontaneously through God opportunities at work, at home, or in the community?
4. How do you serve at the church?
5. Do you find God gives you powers, gifts, and opportunities to serve?
6. How have you been served? What did you think about receiving this gift from others?
7. When you have been served, what was the most helpful about the service?
8. How did you treat the people who served you?
9. How have you served others in practical ways?
10. Have you ministered to others through prayers or gifts of the Holy Spirit?
11. How do you serve your family at home? Is that in balance with your service outside the home? Do you involve your family in your service outside the home or serve together?
12. Do you spend time preparing and training for servant leadership?
13. Do you know how to set your boundaries and say no when saying yes would cause you to be a grumpy servant and not give with a cheerful heart?
14. Are you able to recognize your need to receive and accept being served gratefully?
15. Can you ask for help when needed?
16. Can you lay down your own needs to focus on the needs of others?

AFFIRMATIONS:

- ☐ I am aware of my gifts, talents, and skills as well as God's ability to overcome my weaknesses.
- ☐ I recognize and seize opportunities to use my gifts, talents, and skills to serve others by practicing in the church first and then seeking opportunities outside the church.
- ☐ I can recognize when I need the service of others and understand the blessing I give to them by letting them serve me.
- ☐ I take a break from service periodically to rest and evaluate where God wants me to serve next.

30 DAY PROJECT REVIEW QUESTIONS:
1. How do you currently Minister to Others?
2. What about your current ministries are working?
3. What about how you minister to others needs improvement?
4. List your goals for this area in your HMN.
5. Choose one or two priority goals in this area to accomplish or get started on this week. Write them down in your HMN.

TOOLKIT:
- Service Questionnaire
- Servant Leadership Training

SUGGESTIONS FOR FURTHER STUDY
- *Live Your Calling: A Practical Guide to Finding and Fulfilling Your Mission in Life* by Kevin Brennfleck and Kay Marie Brennfleck
- *The Power of Serving Others: You Can Start Where You Are* by Gary Morsch and Dean Nelson

Forms and Samples

The 30 Day Project Schedule

Sunday	Monday	Tuesday	Wednesday	Thursday	Friday	Saturday
REST	*Review and Set Goals*					Projects
Seek God	Day 1 Prayer Covering	Day 2 Functional Zones	Day 3 Household Provisions	Day 4 Keeping Track	Day 5 Establishing Routines	For Them
	Day 6 Filing System	Day 7 Paying Bills	Day 8 Personal Care	Day 9 Estate Planning	Day 10 Devotion/Bible Study	
Allow God	Day 11 House Rules	Day 12 Personal Space	Day 13 Resource Room	Day 14 Delegating Responsibility	Day 15 Home Maintenance	With Them
	Day 16 Family Communicaitons	Day 17 Simplifying	Day 18 Family Care and Fitness	Day 19 Decision Making	Day 20 Life/Work Planning	
For God	Day 21 Home Vision	Day 22 Activity Spaces	Day 23 Security and Safety	Day 24 Outside Resources	Day 25 Relationships	From Home
	Day 26 Gifts and Talents	Day 27 Hospitality	Day 28 Work/Rest Balance	Day 29 Master Planning	Day 30 Serving	

Form 30HMP – Thirty Day Home Management Project Schedule

The 2 Week Review

Sunday	Monday	Tuesday	Wednesday	Thursday	Friday	Saturday
REST	*Review and Set Goals*					Projects
Seek God	Day 1 Prayer Covering	Day 2 Functional Zones	Day 3 Household Provisions	Day 4 Keeping Track	Day 5 Establishing Routines	For Them
	Day 6 Filing System	Day 7 Paying Bills	Day 8 Personal Care	Day 9 Estate Planning	Day 10 Devotion/Bible Study	
Allow God	Day 11 House Rules	Day 12 Personal Space	Day 13 Resource Room	Day 14 Delegating Responsibility	Day 15 Home Maintenance	With Them
	Day 16 Family Communicaitons	Day 17 Simplifying	Day 18 Family Care and Fitness	Day 19 Decision Making	Day 20 Life/Work Planning	
For God	Day 21 Home Vision	Day 22 Activity Spaces	Day 23 Security and Safety	Day 24 Outside Resources	Day 25 Relationships	From Home
	Day 26 Gifts and Talents	Day 27 Hospitality	Day 28 Work/Rest Balance	Day 29 Master Planning	Day 30 Serving	

Form 2WR- Two Week Review Schedule

Chapter Two Functional Needs Index

Storage
- ☐ Clothes, Coats, & Shoe Storage
- ☐ Tools and Home Repair Needs
- ☐ Household Provisions (paper goods, cleaners, etc)
- ☐ Seasonal Items
- ☐ Important documents

Creativity
- ☐ Memorabilia organization
- ☐ Craft Supply storage
- ☐ Craft project/Sewing areas
- ☐ Music expression/practice areas

Socializing
- ☐ Entertaining Guests
- ☐ Family Time
- ☐ Game Tables
- ☐ Bar or Buffet
- ☐ Overnight Guests

Sleeping/Rest
- ☐ Restful Sleep areas
- ☐ Relaxing locations (hot tubs, hammocks, recliners, gardens)

Office Space
- ☐ Homework/Study areas
- ☐ Bill Paying/Home Management areas
- ☐ Home Office/Work from Home Office

Quiet Space
- ☐ Reading areas
- ☐ Puzzle tables
- ☐ Meditation/Prayer areas
- ☐ Journaling tables

Playing Space
- ☐ Toy areas
- ☐ Coloring areas
- ☐ Work out/Dance areas

Dining
- ☐ Cooking area
- ☐ Dining Room Table
- ☐ Cookware/Table Ware storage and display
- ☐ Vegetable Gardens and Herbs

Chapter Four Samples and Forms

Ref	Tasks	FRQ	J	F	M	A	M	J	J	A	S	O	N	D	Future Date
	Change filter in Heater/AC Blower unit	M	X	X	X	X									
	Clean out rain gutters	A										☐			

Ref	Tasks	FRQ	J	F	M	A	M	J	J	A	S	O	N	D	Future Date
Ginger	Rabies Shot	2yrs.				X									April 2008

Ref	Tasks	FRQ	J	F	M	A	M	J	J	A	S	O	N	D	Future Date
Taurus	Change Oil	Q			X			X			X	☐			
Truck	Change Oil	Q		X			X			X		☐			

Sample 4-2: Task Tracker

Vehicle Year/Make/Model: *1996 Ford Windstar* VIN# _____					
Date	Odomet	Description of Maint.	Service Ctr/Tech	Mechanic's Comments	
12-19-06	65,499	Changed Oil 10W40 Penzoil & oil filter	Joe's Garage/ Bob	R. front tire tread wearing low	
1-6-2007	65,610	Replaced two front tires w/ P125R17	D&D Tires/Mark	Tiger Paws	

Sample 4-3: Vehicle Record Form

Make	Model	Year	Serial #	Warranty Expires	Task FRQ's	Purchase Info (Date/Cost/Whom)	Manual?
Sears-Dryer	KA1667	2001	498	12/14/2006	A	12/14/2001 Sears, Lawrence, KS	Yes

Sample 4-4: Major Appliance List

Common Recurring Household Tasks List: Form 4-1

Vehicles
(Check your owner's manual for recommended maintenance schedule and warranty requirements)
- [ ] Change Oil, Oil Filter, and check belts and fluids (every three months)
- [ ] Check Tire Pressure/Tread and lube wheel bearings (monthly)
- [ ] Rotate tires every 10,000 miles or as recommended.
- [ ] Clean air filters and change as necessary, as recommended.

Structures
- [ ] Clean out gutters (twice a year)
- [ ] Check drains and outdoor water systems (Spring)
- [ ] Change HVQC Air Filters (as recommended, usually monthly or every 3 months)
- [ ] Hose out Air Conditioner Compressor (Spring)
- [ ] Test auto reverse on garage door openers (quarterly)
- [ ] Have Chimney cleaned (fall)
- [ ] Test Sump pump (fall)
- [ ] Test the main water shutoff (twice a year)
- [ ] Spray silicone spray on sliding door tracks (spring)

Yard
- [ ] Trim trees and bushes (once a year)
- [ ] Remove hoses from outdoor faucets and store (fall)
- [ ] Clear leaves and debris from around house foundation and drains (monthly)
- [ ] Clean out window wells twice a year.

Appliances
(Check your Owner's Manual for additional preventive maintenance)
- [ ] Clean out dryer vents (once a year)
- [ ] Clean coffee makers/disposals/dishwashers with vinegar (quarterly)
- [ ] Clean shower heads (quarterly)
- [ ] Clean range hood filter (quarterly)
- [ ] Put yeast in septic tanks (once a month)
- [ ] Inspect and clean out septic tanks (annually)
- [ ] Run water & flush toilets in unused bathrooms (quarterly)
- [ ] Check & add salt to water conditioner (quarterly)
- [ ] Test hot water heater pressure valve (twice a year)
- [ ] Drain hot water heater (once a year)
- [ ] Clean refrigerator drain pan (frost free) (monthly)
- [ ] Vacuum refrigerator coils (twice a year)
- [ ] Have A/C serviced (Spring)
- [ ] Have Heating system serviced (Winter)
- [ ] Pour water down unused drains (monthly)

Safety
- [ ] Inspect fire extinguishers (monthly)
- [ ] Test smoke detectors (monthly)
- [ ] Replace batteries in smoke/Carbon dioxide detectors (twice a year)
- [ ] Test GFCI Outlets

Ref	Tasks	FRQ	J	F	M	A	M	J	J	A	S	O	N	D	Future Date

Form 4-2: Task Tracker

Vehicle Year/Make/Model: _____

VIN # _____

Date	Odometer Reading	Description of Maint.	Service Center/Tech	Mechanic's Comments

Form 4-3 Vehicle Maintenance Log

Make	Model	Year	Serial #	Warranty Expires	Task FRQs	Purchase Info (Date/Cost/Whom)	Manual?

Form 4-4: Major Appliance List

Chapter Five Samples and Forms

Routine Name:							
Tasks to be completed on:	S	M	T	W	R	F	S

<circle days> S-M-T-W-R-F-S	
Times:	Routine:

<circle days> S – M – T – W – R – F – S	*Work/School Days Schedule*
Times:	**Routine:**
AM	*Dish Tour*
PM (after work)	*Clothes Tour (start laundry)/Paper Tour/Clutter Tour (zone defense)*
5:30pm	*Cook/Clean Routine*
8pm	*Bedtime Routine*

Daily Routine Task Schedule and Routine Definitions Sample

Routine Name: *Dish Tour*							
Tasks to be completed on:	S	M	T	W	R	F	S
Empty Dishwasher of Clean dishes and put away	X	X	X	X	X	X	X
Walk through house and pick up all dishes	X	X	X	X	X	X	X
Return dishes to kitchen and load in dishwasher	X	X	X	X	X	X	X
Clear counters of all dirty dishes and load in dishwasher	X	X	X	X	X	X	X
Start and run dishwasher (Each evening or when full)	X	X	X	X	X	X	X

My **EVERYDAY** List

Household chores (2 minutes each)
- ☐ Pick up/burn/take out a pile of trash
- ☐ Clear up dirty dishes
- ☐ Wash/run/put away a load of dishes
- ☐ Gather a load of clothes
- ☐ Wash/Dry a load of clothes
- ☐ Fold/Put away a load of clothes
- ☐ Water/weed/mow
- ☐ Dust Something (table, a bookcase, a piano)
- ☐ Shine Something (a window, a mirror, a tv screen)
- ☐ Disinfect something (a toilet, a counter, a litter box, a cage)
- ☐ Sort/file/act through a pile of papers or incoming mail
- ☐ Update books and file receipts
- ☐ Straighten/zone clean up a shelf, a drawer, a corner
- ☐ Put away some clutter/unpack a box

Ranch Chores (5 minutes each):
- ☐ Throw **AM** hay to stabled horses or turn out
- ☐ Feed/water/hay rabbits **AM/PM**
- ☐ Feed/water dogs **AM/PM**
- ☐ Feed/water cats **AM/PM**
- ☐ Feed/water/hay horses **PM**
- ☐ Feed humans breakfast (toast)
- ☐ Feed humans lunch (sandwiches)

Ranch Chores (15 minutes minimum)
- ☐ Feed humans dinner (salad and meat)
- ☐ Work with a horse (2 hours on RDO's)
- ☐ Enter events in Ranch Log

Personal/Projects (15 minutes)
- ☐ Read a bible chapter or scripture
- ☐ Help kids with homework
- ☐ Write/revise a chapter/article of original work
- ☐ Read a chapter of current study
- ☐ Check email/blog/list (15 minutes MAX)
- ☐ Exercise something
- ☐ Set Launch pad (next day prep)
- ☐ Review business plan or update website
- ☐ Shower

Relax – choose one or enjoy a spontaneous activity
- ☐ TIVO or DVD
- ☐ Visit with someone face to face
- ☐ Play a game of cards with the kids
- ☐ Play the piano or work on a puzzle
- ☐ Read a book

❖ Sample Routine Names and Definitions:

1. Dish Tour

   ➢ Walk through entire house, pick up all dirty dishes and start or wash a load.

2. Clothes Tour

   ➢ Pick up all dirty clothes, start a load of laundry—return in 40 minutes and put in dryer.

   ➢ Fold clothes and put them away

3. Paper Tour

   ➢ Sort through the incoming mail, file in appropriate slot: To Read, To Pay, To Do, File or throwaway.

   ➢ Pick up any pieces of paper, trash, and take out trashcans to outdoor cans or burn pile.

4. Attend Pets

   ➢ Feed cats/dog/ducks, let out the dog, let out/pen up ducks, and feed horses AM/PM, check water tanks and bowls.

5. Water/Weed gardens

   ➢ Alternate days without rain; spend a few minutes picking weeds from one of the gardens—rotate through all gardens at least once a week.

6. Cook and Clean up from three meals and one snack—

   ➢ -Plan and set out ingredients

   ➢ -prep salads and garnishes and condiments

   ➢ -cook main and side dishes as needed—clean cooking dishes as you go

   ➢ ask kids to wash up for dinner

   ➢ -set table and set out condiments, garnishes, drinks

   ➢ call family to table for the evening prayer

   ➢ -set out buffet or serving dishes (serve the meal)

   ➢ -issue clean up instructions

   ➢ -clear table- put away food and wipe down tables and counters

   ➢ -wash, dry, and put away dishes

Chapter Six Filing Index

Drawer One- Finances
- Ongoing Transaction Folders
- Bank Accounts
- Bill Payment Records
- Employment Records (current position)
- Estate Plans
- Health Policies (current plan)
- Income
- Insurance
- Investments
- Rental Records (current tenant)
- Tax Receipts (current year)

Drawer Two- Assets
- Contracts and Warranties
- Computer Settings/Security/Recovery & Back up schedule
- Deeds/Titles -- copies--
- Owner/Operator Manuals
- Property Records (Home, Rental Property, Vehicles)

Drawer Three- Home and Family Management

Home Management-
- Contact Information
- Ongoing Project Folders
- Repair Records- Home, Rental Property, Vehicles
- Resource/Referrals
- Zone Maps

Family Records--
- Certificates (Legal)-- copies--
- Education Records
- Health Records
- Pet Records
- Organizations/Memberships
- Wardrobe lists

Genealogical/Family Historical Documents

Drawer Four- Archives
- Past Tax Returns and support documentation
- Past Health Insurance Policies
- Past Employment Records
- Other Archives

Chapter Seven Samples and Forms

Date	Amount	Where/Whom	Value: Extend to Budget Categories-->	Auto Fuel	Groceries	Bad Habits		
11/25/2016	33.56	Cennex	Yes, Transportation	33.56				
11/25/2016	1.96	Cennex	No, Fountain Drink			1.96		
11/25/2016	6.96	Bob's	No, Cigarrettes, want to quit			6.96		
11/26/2016	115.95	Country Mart	Yes, groceries, meals planned		115.95			
November	158.43			33.56	115.95	8.92		

Sample 7-4: Face It Ledger

Date	Amount	Where/Whom	Value: Extend to Budget Categories-->						

Form 7-4: Face It Ledger

Chapter Eight Samples and Forms

Positive Life Habit	Frequency	1	2	3	4	5	6	7	8	9	10	11	12	13	14	15	16	17	18	19	20	21	22	23	24	25	26	27	28	29	30	31
	Month: January																															
Workout 30 mins	3X/Week		X		X	X				X	X	X	X		X	X			X		X	X		X		X		X		X		X
Cook at Home	5X/Week		X	X	X	X		X		X	X	X	X	X			X	X	X	X				X	X		X	X		X	X	X

Sample 8-1: Habits Calendar

Positive Life Habit	Frequency	1	2	3	4	5	6	7	8	9	10	11	12	13	14	15	16	17	18	19	20	21	22	23	24	25	26	27	28	29	30	31
	Month																															

Form 8-1: Habits Calendar

Replacement Behavior	1	2	3	4	5	6	7	8	9	10	11	12	13	14	15	16	17	18	19	20	21	# of Successes	Reward
Sing instead of Smoke	1	2	3	4	5	6	7	8	9	10	11	12	13	14	15	16	17	18	19	20	21	17 of 21	Buy a new album
Drink Water instead of Pop	1	2	3	4	5	6	7	8	9	10	11	12	13	14	15	16	17	18	19	20	21		Go out for an Ice Cream Cone

Sample 8-2: 21 Day Habits Tracker

Replacement Behavior	1	2	3	4	5	6	7	8	9	10	11	12	13	14	15	16	17	18	19	20	21	# of Successes	Reward
	1	2	3	4	5	6	7	8	9	10	11	12	13	14	15	16	17	18	19	20	21		
	1	2	3	4	5	6	7	8	9	10	11	12	13	14	15	16	17	18	19	20	21		
	1	2	3	4	5	6	7	8	9	10	11	12	13	14	15	16	17	18	19	20	21		
	1	2	3	4	5	6	7	8	9	10	11	12	13	14	15	16	17	18	19	20	21		
	1	2	3	4	5	6	7	8	9	10	11	12	13	14	15	16	17	18	19	20	21		
	1	2	3	4	5	6	7	8	9	10	11	12	13	14	15	16	17	18	19	20	21		
	1	2	3	4	5	6	7	8	9	10	11	12	13	14	15	16	17	18	19	20	21		
	1	2	3	4	5	6	7	8	9	10	11	12	13	14	15	16	17	18	19	20	21		
	1	2	3	4	5	6	7	8	9	10	11	12	13	14	15	16	17	18	19	20	21		
	1	2	3	4	5	6	7	8	9	10	11	12	13	14	15	16	17	18	19	20	21		
	1	2	3	4	5	6	7	8	9	10	11	12	13	14	15	16	17	18	19	20	21		
	1	2	3	4	5	6	7	8	9	10	11	12	13	14	15	16	17	18	19	20	21		

Form 8-2: 21 Day Habits Tracker

Chapter Eleven House Rules

The Ten Commandments

1. You shall have no other gods before me.

2. You shall not make for yourself an idol in the form of anything in heaven above or on the earth beneath or in the waters below. You shall not bow down to them or worship them; for I the Lord your God, am a jealous God, punishing children for the sin of the fathers to the third and fourth generation of those who hate me, but showing love to a thousand generations of those who love me and keep my commandments.

3. You shall not misuse the name of the Lord you God, for the Lord will not hold anyone guiltless who misuses his name.

4. Remember the Sabbath day by keeping it Holy. Six days you shall labor and do all your work, but the seventh day is a Sabbath to the Lord your God. On it you shall not do any work, neither you, nor your son or daughter, nor your manservant or maidservant, nor your animals, nor the alien within your gates. For in six days the Lord made the heavens and the earth, and the sea, and all that is in them but he rested on the seventh day. Therefore the Lord blessed the Sabbath day and made it holy.

5. Honor your father and your mother, so that you may live long in the land the Lord your God is giving you.

6. You shall not murder.

7. You shall not commit adultery.

8. You shall not steal.

9. You shall not give false testimony against your neighbor.

10. You shall not covet your neighbor's house. You shall not covet your neighbor's wife, or his manservant, or maidservant, his ox or donkey, or anything that belongs to your neighbor.

A Simple System of Progressive Discipline

1. Remind the child of the appropriate way to behave.

2. Remove the child from the situation to a quiet, reflective place.

3. Restrict the child to a room or impose limits on privileges.

4. Re-earn privileges, which is necessary for chronic behavior problems. The goal is always repentance, taking responsibility for one's action, and a change of future behavior.

Chapter Twelve Personal Space Balance Chart

Personal Space Balance Chart

⌘ Personal and family time

⌘ Quiet space and activity space

⌘ Personal prayer and family prayer

⌘ Personal retreat/refuge and coming to someone for comfort

Chapter Twenty Individual Development Plan

Individual Development Plan			
For: _____	Created on: _____		Updated: _____
Long Term Goal (3-5 years):			
Short Term Goal (1-2 years):			
Steps to Short Term Goal:	What it will take from me	Resources I will need to help me	Target Date to complete step

Form 20-1

Chapter Twenty One Forms and Lists

Data, Things, People List

1. List your favorite 7 Data, 7 Things, and 7 People groups you like to work with.

2. Number in priority order your Top 5 by criteria such as:

   Sense of purpose/meaning, enjoyment, or seem to have natural talent with.

DATA		THINGS		PEOPLE	

Form 21-2

Action Verbs List

Achieve	Construct	Expedite	Liquidate
Acquire	Consult	Explain	Listen
Adapt	Contact	Explore	Lobby
Administer	Contribute	Extend	Locate
Advise	Control	Facilitate	Log
Advocate	Convert	Finance	Love
Allocate	Coordinate	Find	Make
Analyze	Correct	Focus	Mend
Answer	Counsel	Forecast	Mentor
Apply	Create	Form	Motivate
Appraise	Critique	Formulate	Pray
Approve	Define	Foster	Prepare
Arrange	Delegate	Founded	Project
Assemble	Deliver	Fulfill	Promote
Assess	Demonstrate	Generate	Proofread
Assign	Design	Guide	Prophesy
Attain	Designate	Handle	Propose
Audit	Determine	Head	Protect
Authorize	Develop	Hire	Prove
Brief	Devise	Hope	Provide
Broaden	Diagnose	Identify	Publicize
Budget	Direct	Illustrate	Publish
Build	Disciple	Imagine	Purchase
Calculate	Discover	Impart	Quadruple
Catalogue	Dispense	Implement	Qualify
Categorize	Distribute	Improve	Quantify
Chair	Document	Increase	Realize
Clarify	Double	Initiate	Receive
Classify	Draft	Inspect	Recommend
Coach	Draw	Inspire	Record
Code	Earn	Install	Recruit
Collaborate	Edit	Institute	Rectify
Collect	Elaborate	Instruct	Reduce
Combine	Eliminate	Integrate	Refer
Communicate	Employ	Interact	Refresh
Compile	Encourage	Intercede	Regulate
Complete	Enforce	Interview	Reinforce
Compose	Engineer	Introduce	Renew
Compute	Equip	Invent	Repair
Conceive	Establish	Invest	Report
Conceptualize	Estimate	Investigate	Represent
Condense	Examine	Join	Research
Conduct	Exceed	Launch	Restore
Connect	Execute	Lead	Retrieve
Consolidate	Exercise	Learn	Reveal
Conclude	Expand	Lecture	Review

Revise	Tabulate	Unite	
Reward	Tailor	Update	
Route	Teach	Utilize	
Schedule	Test	Validate	
Secure	Testify	Verify	
Select	Trade	Volunteer	
Simplify	Train	Welcome	
Solve	Transcribe	Win	
Sponsor	Transform	Worship	
Standardize	Translate	Write	
Streamline	Troubleshoot		
Strengthen	Tutor		
Study			
Succeed			
Suggest			
Summarize			
Supervise			
Support			
Survey			
Sustain			

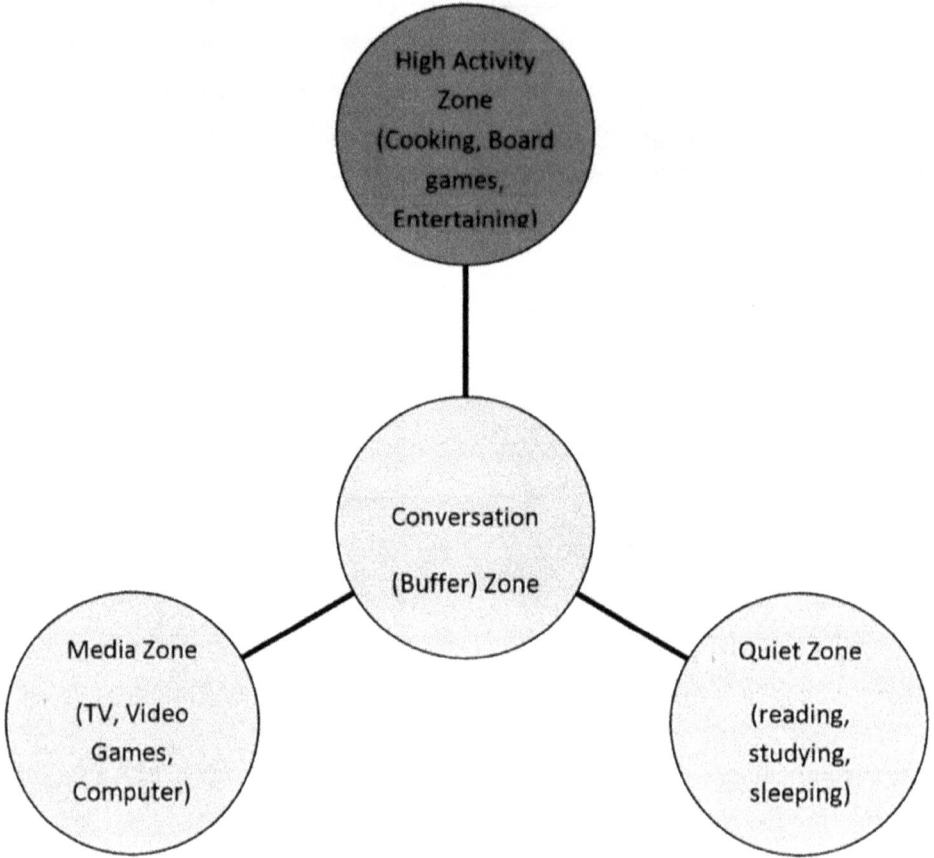

Form 22-1: Activity Balance Wheel

NOTES:

About the Author

K.S. Brixey is an author and *Living Well* life coach in the Midwest. She holds a Master of Science degree in counseling psychology from the University of Kansas, School of Education, Lawrence, KS and a Bachelor of Science degree in Behavioral Sciences from the New York Institute of Technology, Central Islip, NY. She is the mother of four adult children and a grandmother. Dedicated to releasing Heaven on Earth through the Blood of Jesus Christ and Light of the Holy Spirit, her goal is to encourage you to strengthen your Faith, renew your Hope, and discover the True Unconditional Love of your Heavenly Father.

You may contact the author through R4CR Productions, 4000 W 6th Street, Suite B134, Lawrence, KS 66049.

www.ingramcontent.com/pod-product-compliance
Lightning Source LLC
Chambersburg PA
CBHW071433090426
42737CB00011B/1642